The Confessions
of St. Augustine

The Confessions of St. Augustine

MODERN ENGLISH VERSION

SPIRE

The Writings of Augustine

Augustine of Hippo (354–430) was a prolific writer of theological works, covering a great variety of subjects. As in *Confessions*, his fertile mind could drift into very creative ideas on a wide variety of subjects that interested him and in which he always found connections to God.

He also wrote rhetorical arguments on the significant controversies of his day. In particular, he produced a number of attacks on the theology of the Manichaeans, the mystical Eastern transplant into the Roman Empire that had enraptured him as a young man.

A great number of sermons are retained, recorded as was the custom of the period by disciples of the preacher.

The writings of Augustine can be difficult and his reasoning complex, yet particularly in *Confessions* high-toned philosophy gives way to poetic movements of praise and application. He produced *The Trinity*, one of the most in-depth books on the subject ever written, but also wrote sermons that are models of simple communication in the language of the people. A total of 363 sermons have been saved that can be definitely attributed to Augustine. He was trained in rhetoric and taught it, yet as a Christian communicator he believed that emotion-lifting oratory was beneath the dignity of the Christian, who didn't need technique when handling the eternal truths of God.

The following list is far from exhaustive, but it places some of Augustine's writing into his career. Some of these works are among 270 letters and epistles that have been preserved.

368	Baptism of Augustine; *On the Practices of the Catholic Church and the Practices of the Manichaeans*
389–91	*On the True Religion*
392	*Debate with Fortunatus the Manichaean*
394	*Against Adimantus, the Manichaean Teacher*
397	*To Simplicianus*, discussions of miscellaneous questions; *On Christian Doctrine* is begun.
397–98	*Against Felix the Manichaean*
398	*Sermon on Christian Discipline*
398–400	*Confessions*
399	*Questions on the Gospels*

400	*On the Trinity is begun; Harmony of the Gospels; Comments on Job; On the Inquiries of Januarius; Against Faustus*
405	*On the Unity of the Church*
406–12	*Exposition on 6 Questions Raised by Pagans*
412	*Brief Meeting with the Donatists; On the Spirit and Letter; On the Grace of the New Testament; On Merit and Forgiveness*
413	*On Seeing God; City of God is begun.*
415	*To Bishop Jerome; On the Trinity is finished.*
416	*Homilies on John*
417	*On the Presence of God*
418	*Sermons against the Arians; On the Grace of Christ and Original Sin; Reply to the Caesarians*
419	*Questions on the Heptateuch*
419–20	*Against Adversaries of the Law and the Prophets*
421	*Enchiridion, a handbook on faith, hope, and love and synthesis of Augustinian theology*
425	*On the Creed, to the Catechumens*
426	*City of God is finished; On Christian Doctrine is finished.*
426–28	*Retractions*
428	*On Predestination of the Saints*
429–30	*On the Usefulness of Fasting*
Unknown	*Regula ad servos Dei (Monastic Rule of Augustine)*
430	Death of Augustine

The Content of Confessions

Written at some point between 397 and 400, *Confessions* is technically not an autobiography or memoir but a *confiteri*, the praise of a soul. It is one book-length sustained prayer of praise. For this reason, it is frequently misunderstood by those who cannot understand why a book continually addresses God and meanders so freely between anecdotes and theological discussions. Superficially, the first ten chapters seem unrelated to the last three.

A careful study of the subjects and flow of the text, however, shows that the autobiographical sections are not a diary or even so much Augustine's testimony of his dealings with God. Rather, the stories are illustrations—Augustine's vehicle to unwrap eternal realities by noticing how he himself is an example of God at work. He is considering the fabric of God's design of life.

We seldom consider most of these questions because they are bound up in our story, which we are too busy living to analyze. Augustine is trying to cut the binding. This is why the text often seems to settle in some insignificant point or emotion or love and spend considerable time looking at it from multiple directions.

Augustine seems to obsess about flaws in his character or interpersonal relationships. Beyond his evident intense emotional sensitivity, he is teaching himself and us through these passages. Each is intended to force us to look at normal life experiences in a new and fresh way, whether the awareness of an infant or the bonds between close friends or the dynamics of grief at a loved one's death. Augustine wants us to see him as a case study in reality, and he thrusts his mind more and more into this reality in the final chapters of his book.

But beyond even the philosophical reasoning, each element becomes a reason to praise God. Such a combination of personal revelation, meditations, and praise is virtually unique in Christian literature.

This edition follows the abbreviated text as first published by Baker Book House in 1977. It omits large sections of the full text of *Confessions* but samples enough to see much of the exquisite joy being unveiled on each page.

For ease of understanding, paraphrase is employed where the literary Latin used by Augustine does not translate easily word for word into English. Paraphrase has also been employed to amplify difficult arguments, though carefully so as to preserve the thought.

The poetic nature of much of Augustine's text has been broken out typographically to highlight the literary beauty of the thought.

A synopsis of the entire breadth of the text may help readers understand the wonder of this student of God at his window on life:

Book One: Augustine introduces the mysterious pilgrimage of God's grace through his life. He observes infants and uses them to imagine what his own infancy must have been like, his learning to speak, and his childhood experiences in school.

Book Two: Augustine's sixteenth year shows depravity at work in his laziness, lust, and mischief. The theft of some pears leads to contemplation of what the sinner really intends in sinful acts.

Book Three: As a student in Carthage, Augustine kindles an interest in philosophy and a turn from Christianity to Manichaean religion.

Book Four: Augustine reaches adulthood and begins teaching, while sinking deeper into the ideas of the Manichaeans and astrology. He takes a mistress and for the first time confronts face to face the fragility and impermanence of life.

Book Five: Hoping for confirmation of his Manichaean beliefs at the feet of the religion's masters, he instead comes to disillusionment. He faces the vanity of human wisdom and begins to reconsider the religion of his mother. But he also flees her domination for Rome and then Milan. There the great preacher Ambrose forces him to look again to Scripture. Augustine becomes a catechumen.

Book Six: Monnica follows her son and finds him again at the threshold of orthodox faith, while dealing confusedly with the intricacies of adult life. Augustine becomes engaged, dismisses his first mistress, takes another, and continues his fruitless search for truth.

Book Seven: In his searching for truth, Augustine finally leaves the Manichaeans behind and rejects astrology but takes a side trip into Platonism as he tries to come to terms with God's relationship to the reality he sees about him. From Neoplatonism he begins to have a breakthrough in studying Scripture and approaching the truth about Jesus Christ.

Book Eight: He finally comes to the point of conversion to Christ. But he still cannot conquer his preoccupation with worldly affairs and his desires. He is at a point of violent turmoil in which his divided will wars against itself. Finally he overhears a child's song, which sends him to the Scripture text that is able to resolve his crisis.

Book Nine: Augustine resigns as a teacher of rhetoric and prepares for baptism with Adeodatus and Alypius. Shortly thereafter, they start back for Africa. Monnica does not accompany them, however, for she has died, and grief becomes the first trial of Augustine's young faith. He finds the experience far different than in grieving as an unbeliever at the deaths of his friends.

Book Ten: Augustine turns from his story to what it means. First, how do memories retain reality and do they chart a path for understanding God? After an intricate analysis of the self, he applies what he has learned to the meaning of prayer. He also looks again at the big picture of sin nature and the Savior who mediates between God and sinner.

Book Eleven: Past memories, present experience, and what he has learned about the meaning of eternity lead to an attempt to unlock the mysteries of creation. He argues that time and creation are intimately related to each other. In fact, time is a created "thing." But what sort of thing is it? Augustine considers what temporal process tells us about the abiding eternity of God's "now." This gives new insights into the first verses of Genesis.

Book Twelve: Defending the truth of Scripture's account of creation, Augustine wonders at how visible, formed matter came out of nothing. He struggles again with his understanding of Genesis 1:1–2, realizing that he has not considered all possible explanations for the work of God. This leads to thoughts on how to interpret Scripture and why Christians should approach disagreements over nonessentials in the interpretation of a passage with humility and charity.

Book Thirteen: Augustine considers a more allegorical approach to Genesis to illustrate the deeper realities of God's being. He returns to his consideration of a central theme of his writing: What is the image and likeness of God that is in a human being? He ends with praise to God for His work of creation and salvation, and the final eternal sabbath that awaits God's people.

Confession of the Greatness of God

You are matchless, O Lord.

So our praise of You must rise above our humanity.

Magnificent is Your power.

Your wisdom has no limits.

And we lowly creatures aspire to praise You. What is a human being, but a tiny particle of Your creation? Each human carries within the mark of coming death. That mortality bears witness to human sinfulness. It declares to all that You rebuff the proud.

Yet despite our lowness, human beings aspire to praise You, though we be but a particle of Your creation. You awake in us a delight at praising You. You made us for

Yourself, and our heart is restless until it finds its place of rest in You.

Grant, Lord, that we may know which of two things must come first: Must we call out to You before we can praise You? Must we call on You before we can know You? For who can call on You, without first knowing You? One who doesn't know You may come with a false idea of who You are.

Or, is it rather, that we call on You so that we may know You? "How, then, can they call on the one they have not believed in? And how can they believe in the one of whom they have not heard? And how can they hear without someone preaching to them?"[1]

And so we know that those who seek the Lord will praise Him, for those who seek shall find Him, and those who find will praise Him. I will seek You, Lord, by calling on You. I will call on You with a belief that knows You truly, for You have been preached. My faith, Lord, shall call on You, the faith You first gave to me. By that faith You breathed life into me through the Incarnation of Your Son, through the ministry of the Preacher.[2]

❦

For who is Lord but the Lord?
Who is God except our God?
The highest.
The most good.

The most mighty.

The most omnipotent.

The most merciful, yet most just.

The most hidden, yet most present.

The most beautiful, yet strongest.

The stationary, yet incomprehensible constant. You cannot change, yet You change everything. You are never new, yet never old. You make all things new, yet conquer the proud with old age before they know of its approach.

You are ever working, yet ever at rest. You are still gathering yet You lack nothing. You are still supporting, filling, and overspreading; still creating, nourishing, and maturing; still seeking, although You have all things.

You love without yearning, are jealous without bitterness; share our regret without self-reproach; express anger without losing serenity.

When all others fail to finish what they propose, Your purpose remains unchanged. You receive what You found yet had never lost. You are never in need yet rejoice in what You gain. You never covet yet exact excessive payments, so that You may owe. Yet who has anything that is not already Yours? You pay debts when You owe nothing, but in remitting debts You lose nothing.

And what have I now said, my God, my life, my holy joy? What does any mortal say when speaking of You? Yet woe to the one who does not speak, for silence is the most eloquent voice.

Oh, that I might rest on You.

Oh, that You would enter my heart and make it intoxicated, so that I might forget all woes and embrace You, my only good.

What are You to me? Take pity on me and teach me how to express it.

What am I to You that You demand my love and care enough to be angry and threaten me with grievous woes if I don't give it? It is no small woe if I do not love You.

Oh, have mercy on me and tell me, O Lord my God, what You are to me. Say to my soul, "I am your salvation." Say it loudly enough that I may hear.

Behold, Lord, my heart lies exposed before You. Open the ears of that heart and say unto my soul, "I am your salvation."

After You have spoken, allow me to quickly grasp You.

Hide not Your face from me.

Let me die, so that I will not only die.

Only let me see Your face.

Notes

1. Romans 10:14.
2. While some have suggested that Augustine here refers to the "preacher" Ambrose, whose teaching helped bring Augustine to salvation, the context here makes clear that the only Preacher whose words bring knowledge of God and make praise possible is the incarnate Son, Jesus Christ.

Infancy

Narrow is the mansion of my soul.[1]

Enlarge it, so that You can enter.

It lies in ruins.

Repair it.

I know and confess that You will find corruption there that is offensive to Your eyes. But who else shall clean it? To whom can I cry except You? Lord, scrub away my secret faults. Save Your servant from the power of the enemy. Since I believe You, I call to You, Lord, for You alone know.

Haven't I given testimony of my sins to You? Haven't You forgiven the wickedness of my heart? I don't argue with Your judgment, for You are Truth. I fear my own self-deception, for my corrupt heart lies even to itself. I offer no defense against Your judgment, for if You, Lord, kept a record of sins, who could stand?[2]

And yet . . . although I am only dust and ashes, allow me to testify of Your mercy. Allow me to speak, for I am addressing You in Your grace, and not men in their contempt. It is You who should treat me with disdain; instead You approach me with compassion.

O Lord my God, when I came into this dying life (or shall I call it "this living death"), I knew nothing. But Your compassion enfolded me from the start. I do not remember this, but I have heard of it from the parents of my flesh, those out of whom You fashioned me.

You comforted me with the milk of a woman's breast, for my mother and my nurses didn't fill their breasts with milk for me. You gave this food of my infancy through them. This was the result of Your rule, by which You send riches to flow from the hidden springs of creation. You made me so that what You provided was sufficient. You made my nurses so that they willingly gave to me what You gave to them. Theirs was a heaven-taught affection. You made them willing to give to me what abounded from You. The good that they gave to me was likewise good for them, because it was not really from them but from You.

All good things come from You, O God. All that is whole in me is from You. I have learned since my infancy that all that is good, either inside or outside of me, is Your gift.

Every good gift proclaims to me who You are.

As an infant I knew only to suck, to lay back in enjoyment of what pleased me and cry when something didn't feel good to my flesh. I knew nothing more. Afterwards I began to smile, first in sleep, and then while I was awake. I don't recall this. It has been told to me, and I believe it, for I see the same life pattern in other infants.

Little by little, I became conscious of my surroundings. I did not yet know how best to tell of my needs to those who could meet them. My wishes were trapped inside me, and the providers were trapped outside. They were not able to enter into my thoughts. So I flung about my arms and legs and cries, doing what I could to communicate what I wanted. In truth, I could make them understand very little, but that didn't matter to me. If they did not immediately obey, however hurtful or unintelligible my wishes, I became indignant. I was angry that my elders did not submit themselves to me. I demanded service from those who owed me no service.

And when they did not serve, I took revenge on them by tears.

This, I have observed, is the way of infants, and I was one of them myself. Unconsciously they have shown this part of me better than it could be described by the nurses who experienced it with me.

Behold, the infant in me has long since died, yet I still live. No such immature creature has died within

You, Lord, for You live forever, and nothing in You has changed from before the foundation of all worlds.

You are as You were before all happened that we can call "before."

You are, and are God.

You are, and are Lord of all You created.

You abide, fixed forever.

You are.

The first cause of all things that will not abide.

All things changeable flow from the spring of Your unchanging Being. In You live the eternal reasons of all the time-bound things that cannot reason in themselves.

So speak to me, Lord. I stand before You a beggar. Speak pitying words to me, for I am Your pitiable one. Tell me: Were there times of me that died even before my infancy? Who was the "me" who lived in my mother's womb? Of that time I have heard something. I myself have seen women who are with child.

Were there times even before that life, O God, my joy?

Was I anywhere?

Was I anyone?

Of such things none can tell me, neither father nor mother. I cannot observe the experience of others to learn, and nothing exists in my own memory.

Do You laugh at me for even asking this? Do You tell me to instead acknowledge and praise the "You" that I do know?

I do acknowledge You, Lord of heaven and earth. *I do praise You* for assembling the pieces of my being and for the infancy I do not remember. For You have appointed ways by which we can discover the essential facts about ourselves. We can see others and guess much about Your work in us. We can learn much about Your care by seeing those "weak females" who cared for us as infants.

When I had being and life and when my infancy came to its end, then I knew enough to use language to tell others what I was feeling. How could such a thinking, communicating being come to be, except through You, Lord? Is there a self-made man? Or can we look to any other stream of essence and life from which to be derived?

No, only in You, O Lord, are essence and life ultimately joined. You are most high and You do not change.

Nor does "today" ever come to a close for You. Yet because of You each day does come to a close for us. The day finds its closing in You, for it has no way to end unless You uphold that ending.

And since Your own years never come to an end, all of Your years are one "today." How many of our years and our fathers' years flow through Your "today." Your present is the measure and mold for each of our succeeding moments. Many moments will flow by, and each will have the mark of Your mold of being. And through all things tomorrow, You are still the same.

Beyond and behind all yesterdays, You stand. All has been done during Your Today.

Notes

1. Through what seem to be rambling musings on his infancy, Augustine introduces a number of questions about being, time, eternity, and the changeless being of God that will become important in the latter stages of *Confessions*.

2. Cf. Psalm 130:3.

Monnica: His Mother's Care

When I was a boy, I heard of an eternal life that was promised to us because the Lord our God humbled Himself to stoop to our position of pride. From the womb of my mother, who greatly hoped in You, I was sealed with the mark of His cross and seasoned with His salt.[1]

You saw, Lord, the time when I was a boy, that I was suddenly seized by a stomach affliction and nearly died. God, You saw, for You already were my Keeper, how eagerly I sought the baptism of Your Christ in the pious care of my mother and Your Church, the mother of us all. The mother of my flesh was distraught, for her pure heart in Your faith already was suffering the pains of childbirth to lovingly see me come to be born in salvation. She would have hastened to see me consecrated and cleansed by the health-giving sacraments if I would have confessed You, Lord Jesus, for the remission of sins.

However, I soon recovered. That cleansing was put off, since I would again be polluted by sin if I should live, and the filth of my sin would be all the more defiling and my guilt all the more perilous after I had been cleansed. At that time I believed, along with my mother and all of the household, except my father. He did not believe, but he did not turn me from the power of my mother's devotion so that I would join him in unbelief. It was her earnest desire that You, my God, should be my father and take the place of my earthly father. In this You helped her prevail over her husband, to whom she gave submission (although she was the better person) in obedience to Your command.

I beseech You, my God, to tell me if You wish, the reason my baptism was delayed. Was it for my good that the reins were laid down, that I might have my head and run to sin?

Or did you not really let go?

If You did not, why did I hear Your words echoing around me? "Let him alone. Let him do what he wants. He is not yet baptized." In regards to physical health, no one says, "Let him suffer deeper wounds, for he is not yet healed." Wouldn't it have been better if I had been healed? Then my soul's health would have been safe in the keeping of the one who gave it to me. You would have kept me and helped my friends and me to grow in discipline. It certainly would have been better for me when many great waves of temptation washed over me after I grew up.

My mother foresaw what would come. She preferred to expose me to temptations while the clay was still soft, that afterward I might be reworked and cast in the shape of Your mold.[2]

I lay, a wretched boy, on the threshold of an adult world.[3] At this point, I more feared to speak a barbaric turn of speech more than I feared to commit a barbaric act. I feared less to commit a barbaric act than I feared that I would feel envy at those who remained pure.

I say this in confession to You, my God, that I earned the praise of the worldly, for I thought it gave me honor to please them. I didn't see the abyss of depravity into which I fell, cast off from Your sight.

In Your eyes, how could I be any more foul? My life became so low that it was contemptible even to those who were like me. I deceived my tutor, my masters, and my parents out of a love of play. I was eager to see vain shows, and I had a restless hope to imitate the actors.

I also committed thefts from my parents' cellar and table, enslaved by greediness or a desire to give to the boys who sold to me their play, although they liked to play no less than did I. In the games we played, I often sought to win unfairly out of a vain desire to be first, and in that desire to conquer others I conquered myself. I could not tolerate this fault in others, while I was doing it myself. When I detected someone cheating, I was fierce in my reproach of him. Yet if someone caught me and tried to charge me, I argued the charge instead of admitting my fault.

Is this the innocence of boyhood?

No, Lord, it is not.

It is not.

I cry to You for mercy, O my God.

Such sins ripen as the years go by.

Sins against tutors and masters, involving nuts and balls and sparrows, become sins against magistrates and kings, involving gold and manors and slaves. The adult becomes liable to punishments more severe than the rod.

It was not such sins, but rather the humble ideal of childhood, that You, oh King, commanded that we make the emblem of our humility when You said that the kingdom of heaven belongs to such as these.[4]

Thanks would have been due to You, Lord, as most excellent and good Creator and Governor of the universe, if You had decreed only to give me my childhood. Even then there was implanted within me a trace of that mysterious unity from which I was derived.[5]

For I shared in unity with God that I lived, and felt, and had a measure of power to control my own well-being. My inner self tested the truth of what my outward senses discovered. In these little pursuits that occupied my mind, I learned to delight in truth and hated to be deceived. I was given a vigorous memory and eloquent speech. I was blessed with friendship. I was able to avoid pain, degradation, and ignorance.

Didn't I cultivate a life that was excellent and praiseworthy in so small a creature? But no, it was not my doing. All these were gifts from my God—none were from me—in whatever came together in myself.

He who made me is good.

He is my good.

I lay exultation before Him for every good that the boy I was possessed. And for every sin, I find no fault in Him. It was in His creatures—in me and in others—to seek pleasures, to yearn for splendors and subtle truths. So we fell headlong into sorrow, confusion, and error.

But thank You, my joy . . . my glory . . . my confidence . . . my God.

Thank You for Your gifts.

You kept them for me, as You keep me.

Your gifts will grow and be perfected.

And so shall I, until I am with You.

Until I fully know the existence You have given to me.

Notes

1. A reference to a rite then practiced in the Western Churches of rubbing salt on the catechumen upon admission to preparation for

membership, denoting the purity required of Christians. It may in some churches have been rubbed upon young children, as Augustine seems to be saying here.

2. His unregenerate nature, on which the image of God was not yet impressed, rather than the regenerate.

3. In a section not included, Augustine berates himself for wasting his childhood education. He had avoided the Greek poets and their under-standings and run instead after the superficial, immoral, and emotional Latin stories. Augustine never felt that he had an adequate grasp of New Testament Greek. He had avoided learning mathematics and instead ex-celled at rhetoric and declamation, which he dismisses as playing with trifles. His mind had wandered into worthless things, he relates, because he was not anchored in God's Word.

4. Cf. Matthew 18:4; Mark 10:14–15; Luke 18:16–17.

5. Augustine speculates on the extent to which he as fallen creature can share in God's attributes and even His simplicity of being, for His being is without parts and so it is pure beingness. Augustine is not here returning to the Manichaeism that he followed as a young man. He is exploring the wonder of the *imago Dei*, the image of God, imprinted on the human psyche. He explores the implications of unity with simplicity of God further elsewhere: "To be, is no other than to be one. In as far, therefore, as anything attains unity, in so far it 'is.' For unity works congru-ity and harmony, whereby things composite are harmonious, in so far as they are united. For things without parts are in themselves, because they exist in oneness. Things compounded, imitate this unity [that is found only in God] by the harmony of their parts. So far as they attain to unity, they find existence. Order and rule secure being, disorder tends toward nonbeing" (*On the Practices of the Catholic Church and the Practices of the Manichaeans*, chap. 6).

At Carthage

To Carthage I came.[1] There I put my ear to the cauldron and heard from within and all around a song of unholy loves.

I did not love, but I loved the thought of love.

And in the depths of my desires, I detested the fact that I could not love more.

I looked for something to love in my love of loving.

I hated safety and wanted no path that did not have its snares.

The reason was that inside me there was a famine of inward food. I was starving for You, my God. This was not the sort of famine in which I realized my hunger. Indeed I lacked any longing for incorruptible sustenance, not because I had been filled with it, but because I was empty and loathed it. As a result, my soul became feeble and full of sores.

In misery my soul cast about, seeking sensual objects that could scratch where the pox itched. Yet there was no love to be found. None of these things had a soul, so they could not be objects of love.

To love then, and to be loved, was sweet to me. But when I found someone I loved, I wanted only to possess and enjoy the body of the person I loved. I found a spring of friendship and polluted it with lascivious filth. I veiled the brightness of real love with a hell of foul, unseemly lust.

Outwardly my great vanity appeared refined and sophisticated. So I fell head first into the love that I had so wanted to be captured by.

My God, my Mercy, how much bitter root did You sprinkle on that sweetness? You were gracious to do it. I was loved and found a bond of joy; yet with that bond came chains of sorrow. I was beaten with red-hot irons of jealousy, suspicion, fear, anger, and quarreling.

The theater enchanted me with its images of my own miseries. Its plays added fuel to my fire. What makes someone want to be made sad? Why behold doleful tragedies, vicariously experiencing what does not have to be suffered? Yet the spectator wants to feel sorrow at the stories, and this very anguish is pleasure. This seems to be wretched insanity. As more false emotion is elicited by what happens on stage, there is less freedom for one's own true feelings.

How odd that when one suffers personally, it is called "misery." When it is vicarious, it is styled as a sort of mercy. How is it compassion to feel made-up emotions about imaginary acts? The one who watches is not called on to help relieve pain, but only to grieve. More applause is given to the actor who can elicit more grief. If the calamities depicted (whether historical or just made up) do not move the spectator to tears, he goes away disgusted and criticizing. If he is moved to passion, he watches intently and weeps for joy.

Do we really love to grieve? Certainly all want to have joy. No one wants to be miserable. So perhaps it is that we are pleased if we can act with merciful affection. Since mercy cannot exist without passion, we stir our passions for this reason alone. This desire for affection is the channel for friendship. But where do passions take that channel? Friendship plus passion runs into a molten, bubbling, river of pitch. This virtue is transformed by our willfulness into hot waves of lust. Its affection should have the clarity of heaven, but it instead is corrupt when left to follow its own way.

So shall we avoid all feelings of compassion? Certainly not, nor is it wrong to take up a grief out of affection. But be careful of that temptation to impurity. O my soul, whose guardian is the exalted God of my fathers, beware of impurity.

I have not ceased feeling compassion since those days. But then I found my joy in lovers, and we wickedly imagined how we would enjoy one another's bodies, even if only in the imagery of the play. And when the lovers on stage lost one another, I felt compassion and anguish for them, secretly delighting in these feelings. Now I reserve my pity for the one who still finds happiness in such degradation. I feel more compassion for that person than I do for someone whom others pity because he has missed out on noxious indulgences of wretched rapture. This certainly is the truer mercy—not the sort that delights in grief.

However much someone may be commended for loving others enough to share their misery, genuine compassion is not about looking for some excuse to feel sad. If our good will were as ill willed as the mercy of the theater, which of course would be a contradiction, then the one who shared someone's sorrow would want them to be even more miserable, so that he might have more to commiserate with.

Sorrow is permitted human beings, but it is not to be desired if we would be like You, Lord God. For You, who love souls far more purely than we and feel a perfect pity for others, are wounded, yet without sorrow. How can we be like You in this?

It was a sign of my desolation that I loved theatrical emotions, and looked for occasions to empathize with fake, impersonated misery. So I loved acting and was attracted to the stage with a passion, even though performances stirred only tears. Is it any wonder that this straying, hapless sheep, who was dissatisfied with

Your shepherding, was infected with a foul disease?[2] Since I had come to love unhappiness, why shouldn't an occasion for it sink deep into me? I didn't care what I looked at, and I wasn't bothered that I was listening to fictions that only scratched the surface of real life. And so it was as if infected claws scratched my skin and left inflamed, swollen wounds and putrid sores. Was such an existence really a life, O my God?

Even then Your faithful mercy hovered over me, although I had withdrawn far from You. I was busy consuming my own body with grievous sins and pursuing speculative philosophy that dishonored You. Since I had forsaken You, You allowed me to approach the treacherous edge of the abyss. I was lured into the service of demons, to whom I made evil sacrifices. In all this following my own will, I was inwardly feeling the bite of Your whip.

Once I even dared to plan an enterprise of sin leading to death while Your sacrament was being celebrated in church. For that You did send grievous punishments, though I do not blame You, O my God of surpassing mercy. You remained my refuge from the dreadful destroyers, even as I wandered proudly with them and withdrew from You.

How I loved mine own ways and not Yours.

How I preferred my vagabond freedom.

My discipline as a student drew praise, and I thought I could excel as a litigator in the courts. The more my work was praised, the better I became at it. Such is human

35

blindness, that we glory in our sightless condition. I was proud of my standing as first in my class in the school of rhetoric. I swelled with arrogance.

To my credit, You know, Lord, that I avoided and did not take part in the acts of the Eversores.[3] This unfortunate, demonic name was a badge of identity among some with whom I lived. I associated with them shamelessly, although I did not join in their acts. I lived with them and sometimes was glad of their friendship, although I hated what they did. They were proud of subverting the naïveté of newcomers. With their coarse, malicious partying, they luridly disturbed the lives of strangers. No actions are more like those of the devils than their attempts to lure others into wickedness. So what name would be better than what they called themselves—"Eversores"? They first subverted and totally perverted themselves, and the deceiving spirits secretly mocked them, even as they seduced them, while they thought themselves so sophisticated to mock and deceive others.

Confused as I was and living with such people, I studied the great books of rhetoric and dreamed of being an eminent orator. Fame was the goal of my detestable vanity, for I rejoiced in human conceit.

During my studies, I happened upon a book of Cicero. Almost everyone admires his discourses, although not his heart. This book, *Hortensius*, is an exhortation to philosophy.[4] It changed my attitudes and turned me to pray to You, O Lord, with new goals and desires. Cicero taught me that every vain hope is worthless. Suddenly I burned with an intense desire to find wisdom that had eternal value. I began to stir myself to return to You. I did not use that book to sharpen my tongue for oratory, which is what I had been using the money my mother sent to do.

I was then nineteen, and my father had been dead for two years. No, I did not learn from Cicero to use his incisive rhetorical wit. I learned the book's content instead of its style.

How my heart burned then, my God. I yearned to climb from materialism to find You. I no longer cared what You would make of me. For wisdom is found with You, and the love of wisdom is "philosophy," as it is called in Greek.[5] With philosophy that book inflamed me.

Some use philosophy to seduce by disguising error with long words and subtle arguments and honorable sounding names. Almost all who so misused philosophy in Cicero's day and before are censured in that book. I saw as I read about false philosophies that I needed the wholesome advice of Your Spirit, made plain by one of Your devout servants. "See to it that no one takes you captive through hollow and deceptive philosophy, which depends on human tradition and the basic principles of this world rather than on Christ. For in Christ all the fullness of the Deity lives in bodily form."[6] And since at that time I did not understand the Scriptures set down by the apostles, as You know, O light of my heart, I was changed by Cicero's exhortation only to the point that my heart was strongly awakened, and ignited.

I was inflamed to love, and seek, and obtain, and hold, and embrace, not some sect, but wisdom itself—whatever it was.

In the great flame kindled by Cicero's words, only one thing kept me from being overcome. These thoughts of Cicero knew nothing of Christ.

I had drunk devotion to the name of my Savior, Your Son, into my tender heart with my mother's milk. Once I had treasured it deep inside me. And it was Your mercy that nothing except that name had ever taken complete hold of me, however learned, sophisticated, or profound I became.

I resolved then to bend my mind to the holy Scriptures, that I might see what they contained. But lo, I saw in it something that is not understood by the proud, nor laid open to children. Its basic words can be understood by the lowly, but in its recesses are mysteries lofty and veiled.

In my worldly mind, I could not enter into this passageway because I could not bend my head low enough to crawl in. For I did not feel then about Scripture what I can say now about it. Its language seemed unworthy to be compared to the stateliness of Tully.[7] My swelling haughtiness disdained these simple phrases, nor could my sharp literary wit pierce beyond to their implications.

These are words that take root more easily in the hearts of little ones. In my grand learning, I would not allow myself to become small. My swelled head sought greatness.

So I was influenced by men of similar pride, who delight in carnal babble.[8] Their mouths were snares of the Devil, for they mixed in syllables of praise to Your name and to our Lord Jesus Christ, and to the Holy Ghost, the Paraclete, our Comforter. They continually said good things about You, but their desire to praise God went only so far as the sound of the words on their tongues, for they had no truth in their hearts.

Yet they cried, "Truth! Truth!" and spoke about it to me all the time. But their words were lies that had nothing of You in them, for truth is only in You.

Nor did they tell the truth about the elements of the world and all You made in it. Out of love for You, my Father, I ought to have passed by even the philosophers who spoke truth. Your supreme goodness is the beauty of all things beautiful.

O Truth. Truth!

Inwardly the marrow of my soul panted for You when they looked into their many huge books and found various profundities that seem to echo You to me. But was it even an echo of truth? These books were the platters on which they served up the sun and moon.

I was starving for You, not Your works. The sun and moon are beautiful works of Yours, but not even Your greatest works. For the spiritual realm You made is better than all of our shining, celestial, material works. I did not hunger and thirst for even Your best works, but for You Yourself, the Truth, in Whom is no changing, shifting shadows.[9]

In those dishes, they served up glittering fantasies. It would have been better if I had set the sun itself as the focus of my affection. At least it exists and can be seen. Instead, I was falling in love with deceptive fantasies of the imagination. Yet I thought this was Your truth, so I ate of it. I didn't relish this mental food, because it didn't taste of Your reality. In the end You were not to be found in their empty philosophy.

Their ideas were not nourishing, but rather exhausting. Food in our dreams looks very much like food in the waking world, yet the sleeping who taste of it are not nourished. Those ideas I ate from were not at all like You. I know that now, since You have spoken to me. These were like waking dreams, a fantasy of the material in which false images replaced the realities on earth and in the heavens.

We do better studying what our fleshly eyes can see around us, sights that are certain because animals and birds can see them too. The real objects are more certain than the fancies we attach to them.

And again, when we can fix the realities in mind, then we see that the conjectures of them are empty of meaning, for they don't match the truth. Such ideas are empty husks of grain, which I could eat and not be fed.

But in looking for You, my soul's love, I grow faint with hunger, so that I may later be strong. You are not in the material things we see. Although You are in heaven, it is not the same heaven with those things we see in the sky. You created them. Nor do You count them among Your highest works.

How far You are from my fantasies of heavenly bodies that are in no respect like the real ones, even from dazzling images that correspond to bodies that are indeed in the universe of Creation. The fantasies may seem certain but more certain still are the real objects.

What is certain is that they are not You. They have not a spark of life in them.

Better and more certain is the life that is beyond the bodies. It is better than any object itself.

You art that life behind souls, the life that is source of lives, having life in Yourself.

You who change not are the life of my soul.

And You sent Your hand from above, and drew my soul out of that profound darkness. My mother, Your faithful one, had been weeping to You for me more than mothers weep at the physical deaths of their children. She discerned the death in which I lay, because she had that faith and spirit that You give. You heard her, O Lord. You heard and did not despise her tears. Those tears streamed down, watering the soil under her eyes in every place where she prayed. Oh, yes, You heard her.

The vision by which You comforted her permitted her to take me into her house. After a time she was again willing to eat at the same table with me, although the blasphemies I followed horrified her, and she detested my errors. In a vision, she saw herself standing on a carpenter's rule of wood, in anguish and overwhelmed with grief. A shining youth came toward her, cheerful and smiling. Because he wanted to instruct her for he did not need to be told, he asked why she was crying every day in such grief. She answered that she was bemoaning my lost condition. He told her to stop and be content, and to look around and notice that I was with her. She looked around and saw me standing by her on that same rule. What was this but You inclining to her heart? O You, God omnipotent, who so care for every person as though You had only the one to look out for. You look at all humans as if each were one.

When she told me this vision, why did I want to twist it to mean that she should not despair, for she would one day be where I was? Without hesitation, she replied, "No; for it was not told to me that I would go to where you are, but that where I am, you would be also."

I confess to You, O Lord, that, as I remember this, and I have often spoken of it, You Yourself answered me through my waking mother. For she did not even have to think about the plausibility of my false interpretation. She immediately saw what was to be seen and what I certainly had not perceived before she spoke. This assurance moved me more than did the dream itself. By that dream joy came to the holy woman.

She was consoled in her present anguish by seeing that the promise made so long before would be fulfilled so long after. For almost nine years longer I wallowed in the slime of that deep pit in the darkness of lies.[10] I often thought about climbing out of that pit, but each time I was knocked back down violently. All this time that chaste, godly, and sober widow, although encouraged with hope, did not stop weeping and mourning, nor did she stop laying my case out to You at all hours in her devotions. Such You love, and her prayers entered Your presence. Yet You allowed me to remain in and to reenter that darkness.

I leave much of the story untold, for I feel the press of other things to confess to You, and much I do not remember. Yet I do recall that You gave her another answer. That answer came by a priest of Yours, a bishop who had come up through Your Church and knew Your books. When this woman begged him to talk to me, refute my errors, show me the lies and teach good things, he wisely refused. He was able to teach those fit to receive his teaching, but afterward I understood why he would not talk to me. I was yet unteachable. I was still proud of the subtle originality of that false teaching.

She had told him that I was using my rhetorical skills to trap those less skilled with wily questions.

"Let him alone a while," the bishop said, "and simply pray for him to God. He will of himself learn his error and how great its disrespect to God."

He then told her how his mother had been deluded and had turned him over to the Manichaeans to be taught. He had not only read, but had frequently copied almost all of their books. Without anyone arguing with him, or proving anything to him, he had seen that the sect must be avoided, and he had stayed away from it.

When he said this, she was not satisfied, but urged him all the more, with pleading and tears, to see me, and talk to me.

Finally he became a little perturbed at her persistence and said, "Go home with God's blessing. For it is not possible that the son of all these tears should perish."

She took that answer as from heaven (and frequently mentioned it to me).

Notes

1. Carthage was a center for learning in Africa, but it was also famous for its sophistication and worldly temptations.

2. The disease in view here is evidently of the heart, not the body.

3. Eversores. This appears to have been a fraternal club of students who tried to recruit the impressionable new students into their ribald humor and licentious gatherings. Augustine refers to this group in other writings. The "fraternity" seems to have been comprised mainly of students from Carthage.

4. This work by Cicero, written about 50 B.C., was popular in the time of Augustine, but no copies are known now. From references in contemporary writings, it is known that the work praised philosophy as the only source of true happiness, encouraging the seeker-after of wisdom to use philosophy to develop his power to reason and to overcome passions. Its title may come from one of Cicero's closest friends and associates, the orator Quintus Hortensius.

5. The word *philosophy* is derived from the Greek words *philos* ("love") and *sophia* ("wisdom").

6. Colossians 2:8–9.

7. Marcus Tullius Cicero (106–43 B.C.), more commonly known by the name *Cicero*, a Roman orator famous for the power of his Latin prose.

8. The Manichaeans, who taught a blend of Christianity and Persian Zoroastrianism taught by a popular Parthian mystic named Mani (216–ca. 276). Following Eastern thought, Mani wrote in six books that the sun and moon were part of God's plan of salvation, to redeem light, which was held prisoner in matter by the forces of darkness. Jesus had come to release light from matter. Since matter was inherently evil, Manichaeism practiced severe asceticism.

9. Cf. James 1:17.

10. Cf. Psalm 40:2.

The Sacrifice of Thanksgiving

Allow me the grace, I pray to bring to mind the wanderings of passed times. O my God, I would use them to offer to You a thank offering. For what am I without You but a guide who would lead myself to my own downfall?[1] Even at my best, I am only an infant sucking in Your milk and devouring eternal food from Your hand.

But is any man different, who is only a man?

At that time a wise and very skillful and well-known physician put a garland of healing upon my feverish head with his own aged hand. He was not my healer, for only You can effect a cure for this disease by resisting the proud and giving grace to the humble.

47

But did You fail me even by that old man, or withhold the healing of my soul?

As I became more acquainted with this man, I greatly admired his way of speaking and listened attentively to how he spoke. He used simple words in a way that was vivid, lively, and earnest. When he gathered from our conversation that I was studying books on birth astrology, he gave me the kind, fatherly advice to throw them away and not to waste the care and attention needed for important activities on what was worthless.

He said that he had in his earliest years studied to make that art his profession and livelihood. Since he understood the writings of Hippocrates, he thought he would soon master this study. But he had come to reject astrology and taken up medicine instead because he found that it was utterly false. He was too serious a man to make his living by cheating people.

"But you can make a living by rhetoric, so you are in this study because you choose to, not because you need the money," he said. "So you should pay attention to what I say, for I worked to master these skills so I could make my entire living by them."

When I demanded of him how it is that many things foretold through natal star charts come true, he answered that the simple rules of chance that are part of the nature of all things will tend to fulfill some of the predictions. If a man haphazardly opens the pages of some poet, who sang and thought of something wholly different, he will often notice a verse that has amazing parallels to whatever he has been thinking about. This isn't something amazing. It is the soul of the person at work, unconsciously seeking out by some higher intellect to look for answers to direct the actions of the seeker. The answer comes by happenstance, not art.

So You taught me much, either from or through that physician, and You left ideas in my memory that I might examine them later for myself. But at that time he could not persuade me to cast aside divination. Nor could my dear friend Nebridius, a youth who was singularly good and had a holy fear. He derided the whole body of divination. However, I still was swayed awhile longer by the authority of the writers of those books. I found no proof that was certain enough for my standards that what was foretold and came true was the result of chance. Enough predictions that came true seemed to have been foreseen by the astrologers who had been consulted.

During those years I returned to my home town[2] to begin to teach rhetoric, I had made one dear friend in the community who was my age and, like me, was starting out. We had grown up together and had been friends at school and play. But he was not so close to me when we were young adults as he would later become. For true friendship cannot really be true unless that love that is shed abroad in our hearts by the Holy Spirit cements the friends together.

Our friendship was made deeper because we had the same study interests. And I took him away from the true faith. As a youth, he had not soundly and thoroughly assimilated it. I warped him to the same superstitions and malevolent stories that so distressed my mother.

We became of one mind in this untruth, and I became dependent on him for spiritual support. But little did we fugitives know how closely You were dogging our steps. You were at one time the God of vengeance and a Fountain of mercies.

You were turning us to Yourself by wonderful paths.

You took that man out of this life after just a year of friendship, a friendship that I look back on as more precious than any other affection of my life.

Who can do justice to praising You for all the ways You lead us inwardly? What You then did, my God, is incomprehensible in the abyss of Your calculations. A long time he lay in horrible sickness with a fever. He lay unconscious in the last extremity before death. Everyone despaired of his recovery, and he was unconscious when given the rite of baptism. I little regarded that, and presumed that his heart would retain the faith he had received of me, without being affected by anything done to his mindless body.

But it proved far otherwise. For he survived this crisis and began to feel better. I never left his sickbed, so close was our relationship. As soon as I could speak with him—and that was as soon as he could speak—I began to make a joke of the baptism he had received when he was utterly absent in mind and feeling. But now that he understood what he had received, he pulled back from me as if I were his enemy. With a wonderful and sudden freedom, he told me to stop making such comments if I wished to remain his friend.

I was astonished, but I didn't express the amazement I felt until he might be strong enough to speak as forcefully as I wanted. But he was spared my fury so that he might be preserved with You and in the end I might be comforted.

A few days later, while I was absent, the fever suddenly returned in force, and he departed.

In grief my heart became completely dark, and I saw death everywhere. Living in my native country was a torment, and life in my father's house was filled with gloom. Whatever I associated with my friend now became a distracting torture. I sought him everywhere, but he was not to be seen. I hated all places because he was not in them, and I knew that in none of them could I expect him, as though he were alive but absent.

The depth of my grief was a great riddle even to me. I asked my soul the reason for such sadness and why my soul was so torn with agitation, but I heard no answer. If I told my soul to trust in God, that idea would have been rightly rejected. For my most dear friend, whose loss my soul was suffering, had been a real man, a truer, better reality than the phantom god I wanted to trust.

Only tears helped me, for they best expressed the deepest of my affections for my friend.

Now all these things are passed by.

Time has salved my wound.

Let me learn from You, who are truth.

Allow me to set my heart's ear to Your mouth.

Why should weeping comfort in time of grief?

Have You, although present everywhere, cast our misery away from You? Do You remain off to Yourself while we are tossed about in various trials? Yet, unless You heard our mourning, we should have no hope left. Where do we find the sweet fruit that can be picked from the vine of life's bitterness?

Do groaning, tears, sighs, and complaints sweeten our petition, so that we hope You hear us better?

There is truth to this in prayer, in that there is a longing to approach You with grief. But why should grief for a thing lost become overwhelming sorrow?

I did not hold out hope that my friend would return to life.

I did not by tears think to lure him back from the grave.

I simply wept and grieved.

I was miserable.

I had lost my joy.

Or is weeping an expression of bitterness, perhaps to make us loathe the very thing that we once enjoyed but have now lost? Does it help us to feel an aversion to what we cannot have?

Why do I speak of these things? Now is the time to confess to You, not ask questions.

Whatever the reason, I was wretched. Every soul is wretched that becomes bound in friendship to perishable things. The soul is torn apart when the thing loved is lost. The wretchedness was perhaps always there, masked by the beloved thing that has been stripped away.

So it was then with me; I wept most bitterly, and took solace in resentment. I now understand that I had become so degraded that I held my miserable life more dear than I did my friend.[3] Though I might willingly have changed things in my life, I was more afraid to leave behind my proud ways than I was to part with my friend. I do not know whether I would have stopped my divination study even for him. It was related if not a fable, that Pylades and Orestes[4] would gladly have died for each other or together, but to live together was worse than death.

In me there had arisen two feelings that do not fit together. I hated life, yet I was afraid to die. I suppose that to the extent that I loved my friend, I hated and feared death as the most cruel enemy that had left me bereft. I was haunted with its power over all men to speedily make an end of us. This was my state of mind.

You look at my heart, O my God, and see such hidden thoughts as I remember having. You are my hope to clean out all the impurity of such obsessive thought, directing my eyes toward You. You were starting to jerk my feet out of the trap into which I had stepped.

It just did not seem right that other mortals lived on, when my friend, who ought to live on, was dead. It did not seem fitting that I myself could live while he was dead since we seemed to be two parts of the same self. It would have seemed right to say of this friend, "You are half of my soul," for it seemed that we were one soul in two bodies. So without him I felt horribly incomplete, as if I would have to live as half of myself.

Perhaps this explains my sudden fear of death, for I felt that I was keeping half of my friend alive, and at my death he would completely die.

What madness, not to know and love others for the created beings we are. How foolish I was to be so upset about the loss of a human being. I was so distracted with my feelings of pain that I could not rest or listen to the good advice of others. I carried around my shattered, bleeding self. I was sick of carrying it but didn't know how to put it down.

I could not find relief in quiet forests, nor in loud games and music, nor in fragrant spots, nor in parties, nor in sexual pleasures, nor even in books and poetry.

The light itself seemed to cast a pall on life without him, so that everything looked ghastly. Life was revolting and hateful. The only thing that helped was my groaning and tears, but there was little rest in that.

When my soul retreated from life, a huge load of misery weighed me down. I should have raised my burden to You, O Lord, and You would have lightened it. I knew the truth, but I couldn't or wouldn't turn to You. For when I thought of You, You were not God to me.

There was no solid substance to my god. I was looking at a ghost, not the reality. My error was my god.

If I offered to drop my load and rest, it fell through the void, and came rushing back down upon me again. I had put myself into an awful fix, in which I couldn't live or continue to exist.

For where could my heart go to flee from my heart?

Where could I go to escape myself?

Where could I go to follow my own running steps?

And yet I did flee. I left my own country once more, so that I would not be always looking for my friend in places where I would never see him again.

That is why I left Tagaste and went to Carthage.

Notes

1. "To be happy, by his own power, without guidance, belongs to God only" (Augustine, *Concerning Genesis Against the Manichaeans*, 2.5). "He alone is truly pure, who waits on God, and keeps himself to Him alone" (*On the Holy Life*, sec. 18). "Whoever seeks God, is pure, because the soul has in God her legitimate Husband. Whoever seeks of God any thing besides God, does not love God purely. If a wife loves her husband, because he is rich, she is not pure, for she loves not her husband, but the gold of her husband" ("Sermon 137"). "Whoever seeks from God any other reward but God, and for it would serve God, esteems what he wishes to receive, more than Him from whom he would receive it. What then? Has God no reward? None, save Himself. The reward of God is God Himself" (*Narrations on the Psalms*, Psalm 72, sec. 32).

2. Tagaste.

3. "Were any to say, I would rather die than be unhappy, I should answer, 'You speak falsely.' For now you are unhappy, and will not to die, for no other cause than to be; so then, though you will not to be unhappy, you do will to be. Give thanks then that you are, which you will, that so what

you are against your will may be removed from you. For willingly you art, but unwillingly you are unhappy" (*On Grace and Free Will*, 3.10).

4. Versions of the story of Pylades and Orestes II go back as far as Homer, but the best-known version of the Greek myth was a tragedy written by Euripides in 408 B.C. Given Augustine's love of the stage as a child, this is probably the story he knew. Orestes was the son of the hero Agamemnon and Pylades was the husband of Orestes's sister Electra. Pylades stuck with Orestes through many difficulties after Orestes avenged his father's murder by killing the murderer—his mother.

Time Loses No Time

The times of life move on, losing no time along the way. Nor does it ever slow down, although our perception of time may play tricks on the mind.

Life experiences came and went, day after day, introducing new memories and thoughts to occupy my mind. Slowly I was patched up and able to experience old enjoyments once more. The grief gave way.

There were other times of grief, or rather other causes of the same grief. For one reason, sorrow had reached in and shaken my very soul, pouring it out onto the ground. I had set my affection on a person, as if a human being would always be there for me. Yet people die. My life was put back together and given new hope, primarily because other friends supported me. I now set my affections upon them instead of

You—that is the great fiction. The promise of satisfaction in worldly loves is an enduring lie that moves the soul to unfaithfulness from its proper lover. We listen, because it is a pleasant untruth, until we are defiled. I refused to let the fable die in my heart, however often one of my friends died.

But life once more centered my mind in human companionship.

My circle of friends talked and laughed together. We took turns helping each other. We gathered to read enjoyable books.

We joked often and at other times were serious. We could disagree without offending. We reasoned as a man would with himself, and our occasional moments of disagreement only spiced our usual harmony of thought.

Sometimes we would teach, and sometimes we would learn.

We would sorely miss the one who was absent and welcome him when he returned.

Such were the expressions of our hearts for one another. We loved and were loved by those who knew well our expressions and words, the look in our eyes and all of our individual gestures. This is the fuel that heats souls until they melt together, to make out of many one. This is the picture of friends bound together in mutual affection. The feelings become so strong that one's conscience condemns any doubt or critical thought about one of the others that breaks that emotional connection.

We were dependent on each other for our emotional needs.

When someone died in the group, the mourning was a dark sorrow that steeped the heart in tears. All of our congenial life turned grievous. The lost life of the dying worked death in the living.

Happy is the one who loves You.

He looks to You for friendship.

He makes enemies only to protect Your honor.

The one fixed in You sees his earthly loves as beloved in You.

You alone cannot be lost; You only are certain.

Our God are You who made heaven and earth.

You fill them with works of Your creation.

You lose none but the one who leaves You.

And the one who leaves has nowhere to run.

Where is there to hide that You are not present?[1]

Where can one flee except from Your care?

What waits at the destination?

Only You and Your displeasure.

Where can the rebel go?

Can he break Your law without punishment?

Your law is truth, as You are truth.

So turn us, God of Hosts. Stand in front of us and show Yourself to check our headlong flight. Then we shall become whole persons. For You already stand in our path, whatever direction our soul runs. Unless we see You there before us, we will remain welded to sorrows, however beautiful they seem. Life's lovelies have no luster unless You give them, and we enjoy them in You.

For all beautiful things have their moment of newness. They rise and set. They grow, become perfect, then decline and shrivel.

Not every earthly thing grows old.

But every earthly thing crumbles.

Earthly things begin and appear to be.

Quickly they grow to their full potential.

More quickly they fade and are unmade.

This is the law of earthly things.

You allot a portion of time and being to each thing, because it is not the totality of Your Creation. It is just a bit of it. Each thing must cease to exist so the next thing in Your plan can take its turn. All the things You made do not exist all at once. Each takes its turn, passes away, and is succeeded by the next, until all the pieces will someday complete that universe of which each thing is part.

It is the same when we speak. We send forth a succession of sounds, each taking its part in forming symbols that will be understood by someone who is listening. Unless each word dies, the next cannot be perfected and succeed it and make its sound.

Weaned from all passing fancies, let my soul praise You, O God, Creator of all. You did not allow my soul to remain attached to corruptible things with the glue of love, attached to what my senses find pleasing. For things we are attached to go where they will, then they cease, leaving the lover torn with corrupted longings.

Love longs for some object to be, loves to rest itself in the thing beloved.[2] But in things there is no enduring place to lie. They don't last. They run away. And then what will our fleshly senses have to hold on to? Who can grasp such pleasures as they flit by? The fleshly senses are slow and dull, bound to taste and smell and touch fleshly things. They work well enough for what they were made to do. But they cannot lock on to an experience and keep it from running on to its appointed end.

For by Your word each thing is created, listens to your decree for it, and follows the way to its end.

You also must listen to the decree, O my soul. Don't be so foolish as to make so much noise that the ear of your heart turns deaf.

The Incarnate Word has been spoken. It calls the soul back to its place of peace that cannot be disturbed and love that will never be disappointed. Notice what things pass away and are replaced as this physical universe moves toward the completion of all its parts.

"But do you see me going anywhere?" asks the Word of God.

So, whatever else you do, my soul, build your house at this fixed point. You have worn yourself out on worthless things. Now trust yourself to Truth. Know that whatever you take from Truth,

He will not be diminished.

In Truth even what decays shall bloom again.

It will be reformed after all diseases have been healed.

After mortal parts remade.

After their being is bound to Yours.

The final things will not fall away.

They stand fast with You forever.

For God will abide and stand fast forever.

Why are you still following your perverse way of the flesh? Let the wayward soul follow the way of those who have been changed. Whatever you are chasing after with your senses, you are not getting the whole picture. You are being delighted by what is incomplete. What if you were given a new sense in your body, a sense able to see the whole reality, and not just cursed, fallen senses that can only take in a part? Then you would see and rejoice that the present things are passing away. For you are happy that the syllables that come from your mouth fly away, so that more can be made and heard.

We await the completion of one thing that is made up of many things that do not exist together. The whole collection will be far more pleasing than the parts. And far better than the whole is He who made all its parts. He is our God. He will not pass away. Nothing will succeed Him.

If you find physical pleasure in earthly experiences, use the occasion to praise God for these gifts. Turn your love not on the pleasures but toward their Maker.[3] Otherwise, the things that please you will cause you to displease. Love those souls that please you, but love them in God. For people will change and will pass by and pass away unless they are firmly established forever. Love them in Him, and carry to Him your own soul and whatever souls will come with you. Tell the souls, "Let us love Him! Let us love Him! He made us, and He is near." He did not make things and then walk away. He remains intimately involved, and all things have their being in Him.

See Him.

There He is, where truth is loved. He can be found within the very heart, even if the heart strays from Him.

Go back into your heart and find Him, sinners.[4] Wrap your arms around Him who made you and hold tight.

Stand with Him, and you will be able to keep your footing. Rest in Him, and you will find genuine rest.

What difficult roads lie ahead? Where will you go? In that place any good thing you discover will be from Him.

Be warned that a thing is good and pleasant only because it is connected to Him. Use it apart from its Source, and it will come to taste bitter. Since the good thing is His, how can it remain worth loving if you forsake Him to get it? So what is your goal as you wander these difficult, laborious ways? If it is not found in Him, there will be no rest—not where you are looking for it. You can keep looking for it, but it is far from the place you are.

If you seek a happy life in the land of death, you will not find it. Can there be a blessed life, where life itself doesn't exist?

But true Life came down to us and bore our death.

By the abundance of His own life, true Life killed death.

And the voice of true Life thundered.

He shouted to us to return at once to Him.

He called us to the secret place from which he came.

His journey took Him first into the Virgin's womb. There He took up the mortal flesh of human creation. He adopted mortal flesh, so that it might not be forever mortal. He embarked into life as a bridegroom into his marriage, knowing the joy of freedom that a great distance runner feels to launch out on the course.

For He never slackened His pace. He ran on.

And He shouted on.

His words and deeds clamored.

His death and return to life roared.

His descent from the Father and His ascent back cheered.

The Life cried out to us to return to Him. When He did leave the world where our eyes could see Him, it was so that He might return to us in our heart. He left that we might find Him. He departed, and—surprise!—the heart is where He reappeared.

He was not with us very long, yet He has not left us since He arrived. He left from here, yet He has not parted from the world He made. He came to the world to save sinners. My soul confesses that I was one of those sinners, and He healed me, though I had sinned against Him.

You sons of men, how dull-hearted you are. Life descended to you. Why won't you ascend to Him and live? But how can you ascend, when you fancy that you are now on high and you screech against the true heavens?

Come down from your pedestal, so that you can go up, all the way to God.[5] For your attempts to rise against Him have only taken you lower.[6]

Proclaim this message, that sinners can only be carried to the Father after they go down into the valley of tears. You do not speak out of God's Spirit if you feel such a fire of sympathy for the lost that you do not tell them the truth.

These things I then knew not, and I loved these lower beauties, and I was sinking to the very depths.

"Do we love anything but the beautiful?" I asked my friends. "What then is the beautiful? What is beauty? What is it that attracts and wins us to the things we love? Only some grace and beauty can draw us to them."

I studied this thought and noticed that in the body itself is a beauty that relates to the unity of the whole. There is another sort of beauty that relates to how corresponding parts come together and fit each other. An example is the beauty of how one part of the body has its place in the whole body or how a foot is completed by a shoe.

These thoughts came together in my mind out of my heart, until I wrote two or three books on the subject "On What Is Beautiful and Fitting." You know, O Lord, what was in the treatise, for I don't remember. I no longer have that writing and don't know how I lost it.

I do remember about that writing, though, that something led me to dedicate it to the Roman orator Hierius.[7] I did not know him, but his depth of learning was legendary. I had heard some quotations that I liked. But what impressed me mostly was that he had a high reputation among important people. It was notable in these circles that a Syrian trained in the Greek form of rhetoric should develop into a great Latin speaker. He was especially well regarded in matters of philosophy.

From this I wonder about the nature of fame. Someone becomes famous because he gains a measure of love, not because he is recognized in public. Does this love result simply from hearing praise? There is more to it. Rather the passionate regard of one who appreciates the work is infectious. Genuine admiration kindles admiration in others who see the famous person's accomplishment from the perspective of the one who is passionate about it. Love spreads from person to person. Admiration becomes infectious when the praise is genuine. The person who is praising has genuine love, without pretense.

Unfortunately, at that time I chose what ideas and people to admire only by listening to the applause of their fans. I did not look for Your perspective, O my God, although You are the only one who is never deceived.

I did not choose to follow celebrities who had achieved popular acclaim for their skill with chariots or as gladiators fighting beasts in the arena. I had a very different, more serious, love for qualities in which I myself wanted to excel. I was not after the sort of notoriety and love that actors earn, although I still did feel great appreciation for actors. But for myself I preferred anonymity to such fame. I would rather be <u>despised</u> than loved for such abilities.

I wonder what drives human hearts to come to <u>value</u> such diverse kinds of loves? Why, since we are equally human, would I cherish a skill in another person that I would <u>hate</u> to have myself? In fact, I would loathe and cast away the ability if I did have it. It does not logically follow that a good horse is loved by a rider who would not want to be a horse. The actor and I both have a human nature. Should I then admire in another man what I would despise in myself? There is deep mystery to humanity, but You number the very hairs of our head, Lord. They don't even fall out without Your permission. It seems to me that the hairs on a head are more easily numbered than are the feelings that beat with the heart.

In my own heart, it was the master orators that I loved to hear and wished to emulate. It was a mistake to model my life after them. I developed a <u>swelling pride,</u> and I was tossed about with every wind of idea the eloquent teachers championed. Yet You were at work in these interests, secretly steering me into the kind of man You wanted. I know and confidently confess to You that I loved that orator more for the stature of his fans than for what he actually did that deserved praise. Had he not achieved their notice or if these men had treated his words with disdain and contempt, I would never have been motivated to ardently admire him. This would have been so, even if his own work had been the same as it was and the only difference was the feelings of the critics.

See how feebly the soul limps along unless it is planted in solid truth.

I did not see then how Your omnipotent wisdom was subtly turning my thinking. You alone could work wonders in a mind that was distracted into material ideas and loveliness. I set myself up as my own arbiter to distinguish what was real and fitting and beautiful. I set standards for beauty based on worldly ideals and took my cues only from the material.

I studied the nature of the mind, approaching it with false preconceptions about the nature of spiritual reality, so I could not see the truth. Occasionally the weight of truth did thrust itself into my line of sight, but I always turned flitting thoughts to what I thought were substantial—lines and colors and measurable shapes. I had set for myself a skewed measure of reality. Since I could not see the workings of the mind in terms of physical reality, I thought they could not be comprehended.

It is my nature to love harmony and feel a loathing aversion to discord. In the former I saw unity and in the latter division. In the category of "unity" I placed rational logic and nature of truth and all the highest good. But on the other side, I falsely imagined a disharmony in irrational life that had actual substance and that substance in its nature was the worst evil. This idea, that evil amounted to a physical life substance of irrationality, did not come from You, O my God, for from You comes all truth.

In my theory I called the good category a "monad," as if it were a passionless, sexless self. The latter I called a "duad." On this evil side I included anger, violent acts, and shameful lusts. I did not know what I was talking about. For I had not known or learned two facts: First, evil is not a substance. Second, the inner self is not some pure center of goodness.

The truth is that deeds of violence arise from the rational thoughts and emotions that have been corrupted. From these inner corruptions spring brutal acts. The self is stirred with unruly, insolent lusts. The affections of the heart are ungoverned and set on carnal pleasures. These defile actions the way illogical thoughts and false opinions spoil a conversation.

If the reasonable soul itself is corrupted; as it was then in me, it will remain dark unless illumined from an outside light. Only worked upon from outside can the soul become a partaker in truth. In itself human nature has no truth.

You light my candle, O Lord my God.

You cast a beam through my darkness.

You gave us of all that You are, and You are the true Light.

You blaze the way before every human that walks the earth.

In You we see no shades of gray.

In You are seen no shadows of change.

I pressed toward You, and was pushed back that I might taste of death. You resisted my haughty spirit. But what could be more conceited, than that I had the strange madness to imagine that I could be what only You are? That I was subject to change should have been obvious. I wanted to change, to become wise and more virtuous. But I preferred to argue that it was You who were subject to change instead of me. You shoved me back to resist my worthless, stubborn view of You.

I imagined physical forms of Evil, and being flesh myself I accused flesh. I was a wind that blew here and there and would not return to You. I wandered on and on to fantasies without reality in You or in my life. My ideas had no substance. My dreams found no origin in Your truth. They were the product of my desire to be important and devised out of my own observations of material reality. I enjoyed debating with Your faithful little ones, my fellow-citizens. I did not realize that I stood apart from them in exile. I enjoyed prattling on foolishly. I asked, "How is it that God created the soul, but then it fell into error?" By implication I asked, "Why is it that God has made a mistake?" I maintained that the unchangeable substance of God erred in not stopping the introduction of sin. I refused to admit that it was my own human changeable substance that had gone astray. I had decided myself to sin, and now my punishment lay in holding on to error.

I was twenty-six or twenty-seven years old when I wrote those volumes. My high-blown materialist lies swirled around me, buzzing in the ears of my heart. My meditations on beauty and holiness took me right up to Your sweet truth, so that I could hear Your inward melody. I wanted to stop and listen. I longed to rejoice in ecstasy to hear the Bridegroom's voice. I could not; for the noise of my own errors drowned out the sound. As my philosophy hurried on, it felt heavier and heavier with the weight of my pride. So weighed down, I was sinking into the deepest pit.

For You did not yet let me hear sounds of joy and gladness, nor did my broken bones yet praise You, for I had not yet been humbled.

What good did it do me that when I was just twenty years old I read a book of Aristotle, *Ten Predicaments*. I revered the name of Aristotle as one so great as almost divine. My rhetoric master at Carthage and others I counted as highly educated often mouthed this name.

So I broke into a grin bursting with pride when I was able to read and understand Aristotle's reasoning without help. When I talked about the book with others, they said they had barely comprehended it although they had able teachers to explain it verbally and even drew out charts in the sand. They could tell me no more about the flow of thought than I had already figured out on my own.

It was that book which first gave me my ideas about material substance. Aristotle taught very clearly that the human being was made of material substance, and so were the human qualities. The human form could be stated in measures. A man stands so many feet high. Human relationships can be described as substantial fact. We can state that a man is the brother of another. We can say where he lives and where he was born. At any moment we can assert that he is standing or sitting. We can tell of his shoes or whether he is armed. We can say what he does or what afflicts him or any of innumerable descriptive things. These are examples of the sorts of substantial things that Aristotle arranged under his "nine predicaments."[8] Substance was the main predicament.

Did understanding all this make me more educated, or did it hinder my mind? I let my imagination run as I thought about those ten predicaments. I tried to use this reasoning to comprehend Your wondrous, unchanging and undivided Self. I wanted to subject Your greatness and beauty to the same categories that can be used to fit our own bodies. The truth is that the best we can do is relate the things of material reality to You. You are the only subject, in which all things have their being. Your greatness and beauty has no context except for You. No human being is magnificent or beautiful in its own bodiness. If it were less perfect in form or beauty, it would still be a body.

By mixing human and divine categories, I conceived a false view of You. There was no truth here, just fanciful notions that came out of my lowness. I knew nothing of the reality of your highness.

You commanded, and the earth brought forth its crop of both briars and thorns in me. It was by the sweat of my brow that I would eat my bread.

What did it profit that I read the greatest human ideas of the so-called "liberal arts" in the books I got hold of. My thinking was enslaved to corrupt desires, so what difference did it make that I could read and understand these books? I delighted in learning, but I had no divine context for what my mind picked up. I had no foundation to discern what is true or certain. I was standing with my back to the light, so that the things that should be illuminated were in shadow, even though they were in front of my face.

Oh, Lord, You blessed me with the gift of quick comprehension, that I could easily understand any book

I came across, whether on rhetoric, logic, geometry, music, or mathematics. But You know that I did not offer these gifts back to You. I used my intelligence selfishly. It didn't benefit me. Instead, it became detrimental. My goal was to use my ability to afford things to own. I did not use my talents for You, so I wandered from You into a far country, to spend Your grace upon my lusts. What did it profit me to have good abilities if I did not employ them to good uses? It was hard to understand that other students, even gifted ones, had to work much harder than I did to learn until we studied together. Then only the ones who most excelled could keep up with me.

Thus it is to my shame that my reasoning brought me to worthless ideas about You. I actually came to imagine that You, the infinite God of truth, had a vast, shining substantial body, and that I was myself a piece of it. That is the height of perversity, but it is where I was. I was not ashamed then to teach and write my blasphemies to others, so now I will not be ashamed to confess that I distorted Your mercies. I was like a dog, barking against You.

What good was my nimble wit in the sciences and my ability to unravel the mental knots in all those volumes without help? I misused knowledge in so vile a fashion that I turned the teaching of faith into a shameful sacrilege. Were those whose minds did not run so fast at any disadvantage, for these faithful ones did not depart so far from You. They remained in the nest of Your Church. There they were secure until they could have all their feathers and strong, well-nourished wings because they ate the solid food of faith.

O Lord our God, under the shadow of Your wings let us hope in Your custody.

Carry us when we are little. Bear us when our hair is white and we cry out in infirmity.

When You grasp us, the grip is firm. When we try to sustain ourselves, the grasp is feeble.

The only good we can know rests in You. When we turn from the good, You push us aside until we return.

Oh, Lord, turn us, lest we be overturned.

Be the good in us that is not corrupted. You are our incorruptible good.

In You we do not fear that there will be no home to return to if we wander off. While we are away, You preserve our mansion with a patience that stretches into eternity.

Notes

1. Cf. Psalm 139:7–12.

2. "In this life men, with much toil, seek rest and freedom from care, but through perverse longings they find it not. They wish to find rest in things which rest and abide not, and these, since they are withdrawn by time and pass away, harass them with fears and sorrows, and will not let them be at rest" (*On the Catechizing of Beginners*, sec. 14).

3. "Wherever you turn, He speaks in the tracings He has etched upon His works, and by the very forms of outward things you remember, when sinking down to things outward.... Woe to them who leave You as their guide, and go astray in the traces of You, who, for You, love the indicators of You, and forget what You mean us to understand by them, O Wisdom, You

most sweet light of the cleansed mind! for You never stop giving us clues of what and how great You are, and these intimations of You are wrapped in the universal beauty of creation" (*Grace and Free Will*, 16).

4. "Because men, seeking things without, become estranged even from themselves, the written law also was given to them; not because it was not already written on their hearts but because they had strayed as a vagabond from their hearts. So He, who is everywhere, laid hold on you, and recalled you to return to your own inner self. What then does the written law cry aloud to those who have forsaken the law written on their hearts? 'Return to your hearts, you transgressors.' What then you would not have done to you, do not do to another. You decided that it is evil, in that thou do not want to endure it, and the inward law, written on your very heart, forces you to know this. You did it, and men groaned at your hands. How are you forced to go back into your own heart, when you endure it at the hands of others" (*Narrations on the Psalms*, Psalm 57, sec. 1).

5. "It is a perverted loftiness, when men reject foundational principles for truth and lay their own subjective base. . . . There is then, strange to say, something in humility that raises the heart and something in elation that sinks it. . . . A reverent humility recognizes who is higher; but nothing is higher than God; and so humility, which makes the person subject to God exalts humanity. But a faulty elation, in that it rejects this subjection, sinks down from Him, than whom nothing is higher, and thereby becomes lower" (*City of God*, 14.13).

6. "By the lowliness of repentance the soul recovers her high estate" (*On Grace and Free Will*, 3.5). "He made a way for us through humility; because through pride we had departed from God, we could not return but through humility, and through One to be the pattern for us that we lacked. For the whole mortal nature of man was swelled with pride. . . . Lest then men should disdain to follow a humble man, God humbled Himself; that even the pride of the human race might not disdain to follow the track of God" (*Narrations on the Psalms*, Psalm 33, sec. 4).

7. Hierius was a relatively common given name in the period, and no one knows the details of this orator. Pappus of Alexandria, a Greek mathematician who died in 350, speaks of a philosopher friend named Hierius, but little is known of Pappus and nothing of his friend.

8. All the relations of things were comprised by Aristotle under nine heads: (1) quantity; (2) quality; (3) relation; (4) action; (5) passion; (6) where; (7) when; (8) situation; (9) clothing. These were all set under a tenth heading of "substance."

Healing and Refreshment

Accept a sacrifice of confession.

You formed my tongue. You stirred it to confess You.

Now may this service of speech give You glory.

You have healed my shattered bones. Let them ask the question of praise: "Who is like You, O Lord?"

He who confesses to You, does not reveal any personal details You didn't already know. You know every thought of every life, for the shuttered heart does not lock You out. The hardest heart can't turn the blade in Your hand. You melt the defenses erected against You by a glance from Your will, either in pity or in vengeance. Nothing can escape Your heat.

But let my soul praise You, that it may love You.

Let it confess back Your mercies to You, that it may praise You.

So long as Your creation continues, voices of praise are never silent.

The spirit of man with voice directed unto You.

The creature animate or inanimate whose voice meditates.

Souls that from weariness arise to lean on what You have created, and then stagger on toward You Yourself.

You made all things wonderfully, with springs of refreshment and strength.

Let the restless and godless just try to leave and run where You can't reach them. You see them, cutting through the darkness. The rebel heart is debased, but the universe all about remains Your lovely creation.[1] How have the godless injured You?[2] How have they disgraced Your government? From highest heaven to lowest earth, it is just and perfect. So where is there any place to hide in which Your presence is not evident? Where can they go that You will not find them?

❧

Truly the sinners flee so that they do not have to see You seeing them. They run because they are blind and they are afraid they might stumble against You in the dark. That is something to fear, for You forsake nothing that You have made. So the unjust do blunder upon You, and they are justly injured in the collision. They have withdrawn from Your gentleness and stumbled into Your justice. They trip over their own worthlessness.

Humankind is truly ignorant if it doesn't know that You are everywhere. You haven't missed anywhere. You alone are near, even to those who think they are far from You.

Let them then be turned and seek You. They may have forsaken their Creator, but that doesn't mean You have forsaken Your creation.

Let them be turned and seek You. There You are in the heart, in the hearts of those who confess to You, who cast themselves upon You, who weep in Your bosom, repenting of their tempestuous ways. Then You gently wipe away their tears, until they weep the more for joy. For You alone, Lord, made them. You are their first cause, not any acts of flesh and blood. You made them, Lord, and You alone can remake and comfort them.

Sinners will not find You on their own, for they do not know the way. They may study to learn about the universe You made. They sense Your presence in what they study and in the mind itself, by which they try to perceive what Your wisdom has wrought.

So the Only Begotten became for us wisdom, righteousness, and sanctification when He was one of us and paid His tribute to Caesar—undertaking all the human experience.

Sinners did not know the way to You from themselves. Now they can ascend to You by way of You.[3]

∽✢∾

They knew not the way, but imagined themselves exalted to the stars. See how they fell to earth, and became fools sitting in the dark.

They are able to say many things about their fellow creatures, yet they do not seek truth from the Maker of creatures. So they come no closer to Him.

Knowing Him to be God, they do not give Him due glory.

They gave no thanks.

So their wonderful words amount to senseless fancy.

They imagine themselves wise. They put on the attributes that belong to You only.

They impute to You what is in them.

Forging lies about You who are Truth, they bind themselves to obstinate perversity.

Thus they changed the glory of the incorruptible God into an image like that of corruptible man, and birds, and four-footed beasts, and creeping things. Trading Your truth for a lie, they worshipped and served the creature rather than the Creator.

∽✢∾

For almost all the nine years in which my unsettled mind had listened to the teachings of the Manichaeans, I had intensely desired to meet Faustus. None in the sect in which I happened to affiliate were able to answer my objections about points of belief. So I held out hope that if Faustus came we could confer, and my difficulties would quickly be resolved. Then he came. I found him to be pleasant to talk to and a man who could speak in more eloquent language. But he said the same things that the other Manichaeans said. I was thirsty, and he was a scintillating cup-bearer.

But I had hoped for a better drink. My ears were already clogged with these ideas, and they didn't seem any better for being said better. These words had no ring of truth behind their eloquence, nor was the soul made wise by the grand presentation and graceful delivery. Those who had held him up as understanding and wise were not good judges. They simply liked to listen to him.

I have observed that a portion of the people will be suspicious of truth and refused to accept it, unless it is delivered in a sophisticated and exuberant presentation. I was saved from the speaker's charm because You, O my God, had already tuned my ear to truth in wonderful and secret ways. I believe You taught me, so that I could discern what is the truth. Beside You there is no other suitable teacher of truth, wherever or whenever a star might seem to shine down upon us. From You I now learned that nothing is any more true because it is eloquent. Nor is anything any more false because it is explained through inelegant lips. Language is rich. Wisdom and folly are wholesome or unwholesome food, however, whether served on a regal or a rude platter.

Whatever the skillfulness of the phrases that garnish it, either kind of meat can be served up on either kind of dish.

After so eagerly anticipating his coming for so long, I was at first entranced by his stage presence and his vitality when debating. Choice and ready words clothed his ideas. I was delighted and complimented and applauded him even more than did the others. It bothered me, though, that when he gave his presentations I could not stand up and ask the questions that troubled me and engage him in discourse. That meant that my friends and I had to get his attention at other times, when it was appropriate for him to discuss such things with me. In these conversations he quickly showed himself to be utterly ignorant of the liberal arts, except for grammar. His knowledge of grammar was only average. He had gained a certain eloquence from reading some of Tully's *Orations*, a very few books of Seneca,[4] some things of the poets, and the few Manichaean volumes in Latin. He had practiced daily until he could speak in a pleasing and attractive manner, and his good wit added a natural grace.

This is how I remember my time with Faustus, Lord and Judge of my conscience. Before You my heart and memory are open. You started then to direct my thinking by Your mysterious providence. You set those shameful errors of mine in front of my face and forced me to look closely at them, so that I might recognize them for what they were and learn to hate them.

When it turned out that he was ignorant of the very arts in which I thought he excelled, I began to despair that he could take apart and solve the difficulties that bothered me. However ignorant, he could have grasped the truths of faith had he not been a Manichaean. Their books are full of rambling fables about the heavens and the stars, sun, and moon. I no longer thought him able to give satisfying explanation of the differences between the calculations I read in science and those I read in the books of the Manichaeans. Was one set or the other more accurate, or was one just as good as the other?

When I proposed that we should consider such things he became quite modest and demurred from the burden. He was aware that he knew nothing about such things and quickly admitted it. At least he was not one of those talkative people I have frequently had to endure who undertake to teach many things and say nothing. This man had a heart, though it was not right toward You. He did not fall into treacherous pits in debate because he knew his own limitations. He would not rashly become entangled in a dispute from which he could not extricate himself easily.

For this I liked him the better. The modesty of a mind that tells itself the truth is better than knowledge of the mysteries I was looking for. I found him open and candid each time I posed a more difficult and subtle question.

This experience blunted the edge of my zeal for the writings of the Manichaeans. I doubted I would find another of their teachers who could answer the various things that perplexed me. I had now met one of their most celebrated teachers. I tried to talk with him about other literature that he professed to know something about and that I was then reading and teaching young students at Carthage. I read to him what he wanted to hear or what I judged that he could understand. I then came to give up totally my plan to advance as a Manichaean by learning profound things from this man.

I did not immediately break all ties with them, however. The truth was, I knew of nothing better. I decided to remain content with the association I had fallen into until something better chanced to come my way.

That is how Faustus, who was to many a deadly snare, unwittingly began to loosen me from the errors I had taken up. Your hands were doing the secret work of Your providence, oh my God. You didn't forsake my soul. My mother's heart's blood was poured out through her tears night and day as a sacrifice for me to You. You did deal with me in incredible ways. I know it was You who did it, my God, for each person's steps are ordered by the Lord to the end the Lord has set. How shall we obtain salvation unless Your hand does the work of re-making what was made?

You directed my way so that I should be persuaded to go to Rome to teach what I had been teaching at Carthage. The deepest recesses of Your wisdom and Your present mercy must be considered and confessed when I remember how I was persuaded to go. My friends did not persuade me to go to Rome by the argument that I could earn more or have higher status, although these things were of interest. The main and almost sole reason I went was that I heard that young men could pursue serious scholarship there with less distraction. The atmosphere of education was more restrained and disciplined. Students could not on a whim drop in to study at a school where they had not been admitted. Students were not even admitted to a class without the instructor's permission. This is far different from Carthage, where a most disgraceful permissive attitude prevails among the scholars. They dare to burst into classes loudly and with wild gestures that will disturb all the order that has been established for the good of his scholars. Students behave outrageously and with amazing indifference to the legal consequences. Custom actually encourages them to act in a more miserable manner. They can do lawfully what Your eternal law declares shall never be lawful. They think they bear no consequences, but in fact they are punished with the very blindness that causes them to act this way in the first place, and they suffer incomparably worse than they think.

I would never have acted this way when I was a student, but now that I was a teacher I was expected to endure it in others. I was very happy to go somewhere that everyone assured me was far different. It was You, my refuge and portion in life, who goaded me at Carthage so that I might change my earthly dwelling for salvation of my soul. You tore me from

Carthage by the special allurements that Rome offered a serious scholar. That is how You draw us to Your appointment. Some men move about frantically, in love with this dying life. Others go after quieter worthless promises. You moved to correct my steps by using my own individual kind of perversity. They who disturbed my quiet were blinded with a disgraceful frenzy, and they who invited me elsewhere savored no less the earth. And I went where I thought I could have less of the misery I hated and more of an unreality that I thought would be happiness.

You knew why I was really going, O God, but You didn't tell me or my mother. She loudly grieved and bewailed my journey and followed me as far as the sea. There I deceived her, for she wanted to hold me by force, either to keep me back, or go with me. I pretended that I would visit with a friend until he had a fair wind to sail. I lied to my mother and escaped. For this lie You have mercifully forgiven me. Full of such awful defilement, You preserved me through the water of the sea voyage so that I could know the water of Your grace. By that cleansing water the streams of my mother's eyes would be dried, for she daily watered the ground under her face for me.

Since she refused to return without me, I barely persuaded her to stay that night in a place hard by our ship where was a place of prayer in memory of the blessed Cyprian.[5] That night I secretly departed, leaving her behind in her weeping and prayer.

What was she asking of You in her tears, O Lord, but that You would stop me from sailing? You, in the depths of Your plan, heard her prayer and knew its main desire. You acted to answer by making me what she had always asked for. The wind blew and swelled our sails and withdrew the shore from our sight. And the next morning she stood on shore, frantic with sorrow, and filling Your ears with complaints and groans. For a while You would disregard them while I followed my desires and You hurried me on to the end of all desire. Certainly her earthly affection for me was chastened by the scourge of sorrows. She loved my being with her, as mothers do. She loved it more than most. At that moment she could not know that You were about to work great joy for her out of my absence.

She didn't know, so she did weep and wail. By this agony there appeared in her the inheritance of Eve. In sorrow she longed for what she had brought forth in sorrow. After accusing me of treachery and hard-heartedness, she began once more to intercede to You for me.

She went home, and I went to Rome.

Rome received me as I was feeling my own scourge of bodily sickness. I felt I was going down to hell, carrying all the sins I had committed against You, myself, and others. I had many and grievous sins to consider, besides that bond of original sin in which we all die in Adam. You had not yet forgiven me of any of these things in Christ. I did not yet have freedom from the enmity my sins had incurred, the enmity Christ abolished by His cross. How could He atone for my sins, for I believed his crucifixion to have been that of something without true flesh? My soul was so dead that it seemed that His flesh was false. It was His death that was true. The life of my soul, which didn't believe, was the real fake.

As my fever rose, I was about to depart from You forever. If I had then parted with life, I would have departed into fire and torment, such as my misdeeds deserved in the truth of Your decree.

My mother knew nothing of my sickness, yet she was praying for me in my absence. You, who are everywhere present, were immediately where she was to hear her, and, where I was. You had compassion upon me, that I should recover physical health, although my disobedient heart was still frenzied. For I did not in all that danger desire Your baptism. I was more intelligent as a boy, when I begged for it and my mother's piety. This I have already recounted and confessed. But I had grown up to my own shame, and I madly scoffed at the prescription of Your medicine. Yet You did not allow me to die a double death in this state. If my mother's heart had been pierced with that wound, it could never have healed. For I cannot adequately describe her love for me, nor how she gave deeper anguish in labor for my birth in the spirit than when she bore me in the flesh.

Knowing the fullness of her love, I do not see how she should have been healed, had I died at that time. What would have come of all her strong and unceasing prayers that constantly lifted to You alone? God of mercies, could You have despised the contrite and humbled heart of that chaste and sober widow? She did merciful deeds continually to serve Your saints. No day passed when she did not bow at You twice, morning and evening. She never stopped coming to Your church, nor did she go to hear idle gossip and old wives' tales. She went to hear You in Your words and speak to You in her prayers. Could You have ignored and failed to come to the aid of the tears of such a woman? She never begged for gold or silver or any temporary, passing good. She begged for the salvation of her son's soul. It was Your gift that she was the way she was.

No, You could not have, Lord. Yes, You were near to her, listening and working the plan that You had determined would happen from the start. You would never have deceived her in Your visions and answers, only some of which I have mentioned. Her faithful heart grabbed hold of each promise, and she always continued praying, urging You to be faithful to what You had shown her, as if it were Your signed contract. For You establish a trust relationship with those who have experienced Your eternal mercy. You have forgiven all their sins and they look to You to keep all Your promises.

You healed me of that sickness. You healed me as the son of Your servant girl. You extended the time he might live in the body until You should give him a greater and longer-lasting wholeness.

In Rome, I joined the same "holy ones" who were deceived and were deceiving others. I fell ill and convalesced in the home of one of the disciples of this group. But I went beyond even discipleship and entered the inner circle, who call themselves "the elect." I still believed that it is not we personally who sin. Rather, I wanted to believe that a foreign force of evil sins in us. That pleased my pride because then I was not responsible. If I did something evil, I didn't have to admit that I had done anything wrong. You would heal my soul because some "it" over which I had no control was responsible. I loved to excuse myself and to accuse some other mysterious "thing" inside me that was disconnected from the real me. In truth it was wholly me and my wicked heart that divided me from myself. My sin was all the more hopeless because I did not judge myself to have any guilt.

What an abominable sinner I was. I would rather have lordship over You, O God Almighty, even if it meant my ultimate destruction, than depend upon You for salvation. You had not yet put your guard on my mouth to lock my lips. I continued to say wicked things and try to justify myself so I wouldn't have to face the guilt for my sins.

That is the way with those who live in sin. And I was one of their "elect."

Notes

1. "As a picture in which a black coloring occurs in its proper place, so is the universe beautiful, if any could survey it. Its beauty is not spoiled by

the presence of sinners, although when seen from the standpoint of truth, they are hideously deformed" (*City of God*, 11.23).

2. "Persons are in Scripture called the enemies of God, who, not by nature but by sins, oppose His government. They cannot injure Him, but they can hurt themselves. They are enemies in that they will to resist, not that they have the power to hurt" (*City of God*, 12.3).

3. "He is the home to which we go, He the way whereby we go; go we by Him to Him and we shall not go astray" (Sermon 92). "Christ, as God, is the home to which we go; Christ, as man, is the way whereby we go" (Sermon 123). "Christ carries us on, as a leader, carries us in Him, as the way, carries us up to Him, as our home" (*Narrations on the Psalms*, Psalm 60, sec. 4).

4. Lucius Annaeus Seneca (4 B.C.–A.D. 65), playwright, orator, and philosopher. He served as tutor to the young Nero and was a calming influence on Nero as emperor. In 65, however, Nero suspected him of plotting a coup and forced him to commit suicide.

5. Cyprian Thascius Caecilius (c. 200–258) was bishop of Carthage and a martyr of the Valerian persecution.

Monnica at Milan

You were my hope when I was a child. Where were You in my heart when I was grown? Hadn't You made me? Hadn't You set me apart from the animals in the fields and the birds in the air? You supposedly made me more intelligent than they, so why did I keep walking in dark, slippery places? I looked for You everywhere outside myself. I looked everywhere for God except my heart. I was looking in the depths of the ocean. I didn't trust the truth. I didn't think I would ever find it.

Soon my mother caught up with me. She had remained steadfast in her faith. She had followed me over sea and land, trusting You to keep her through dangers. She was in danger at sea, and she encouraged the seamen, although it is usually the mariners who have to comfort the passengers who aren't used to sailing. Mother assured the mariners that the ship would arrive safe. She told them that You had promised her of a safe journey's end in a vision.

When she reached me I was in danger of great despair that I would ever find the truth. I announced to her that I was no longer a Manichaean, but I did not yet accept her orthodox Christian faith. She was not as overjoyed at this news as I expected. She knew she had seen me through that miserable existence, and she had grieved for me as if I were dead during these years. She had waited for me to be reawakened. It was as if I lay in death in her mind. She had waited for You to carry me from this tomb, to say to the son of the widow, "Young man, I tell you to arise!" And immediately the dead son would return to life and begin to speak and be returned to his mother.

She displayed no boisterous jubilation, though, when she heard that what she had asked of You every day with tears was on the way to being answered. Although I had not yet attained the truth, I had escaped the chief lie that had held me back. She was totally calm, though, for she had been utterly certain that You would give to her all that You had promised one day. She had rested in full confidence in the Lord. She explained that she had accepted as a certainty that before her death she would see me come to orthodox faith. This had been her serene conviction, even as she poured out her overflowing prayers and tears to You, the Fountain of mercy.

She had cried that You would hasten to set the light in my dark world.

Mother hurried all the more eagerly to the church and listened intently to the words of Ambrose. He was praying that the water of eternal life would gush forth. She loved that pastor as though he were an angel of God, because You had already used him to bring me to the state of doubting faith I had reached. She confidently assumed that I would quickly pass into complete spiritual health through some last convulsion, as a doctor might describe the last crisis of my soul sickness.

In Africa, my mother had taken part in the practice of bringing offerings of cakes, breads, and wine to the church in honor of the saints. When she did that now, the doorkeeper turned her away. When she learned that the bishop had forbidden this practice, she embraced his wishes obediently and even energetically. I was surprised how quickly she rejected this custom, without even asking the reason why she couldn't do it.

Drinking wine had never been an addiction for her. Nor did love of wine provoke her to hate the truth, as it does too many men and women who reject sober teaching the way an alcoholic rejects wine mixed with water. When she had brought her basket to the saint festival, filled with the customary foods, she only tasted herself and gave the rest away. Out of courtesy she would drink a small cup of wine that was diluted to her own temperate taste. And if there were other churches of the departed saints, she went around to each in the same way, carrying the same cup of wine, until the drink became very diluted and warm from being carried about. She would drink with those around her in small sips; sharing in their devotion but not the pleasure. Now she found that this custom was forbidden by the famous preacher and saintly pastor. It was denied even to those who would participate soberly so that it wouldn't become an occasion for those given to drunkenness to drink to excess. These anniversary observances of the saints' deaths did sometimes resemble the superstitious processions of the unbelievers, so she most willingly refrained from them. Instead of a basket filled with fruits of the earth, she took to the churches of the martyrs a heart that was full of pure requests for God. She still gave what she could to the poor; so the sacrament of the Lord's Body might be celebrated fully. These ceremonies remembered that the martyrs had followed the example of Christ's Passion as they were sacrificed and crowned.

It seems to me, O Lord, and I believe in my heart before You, that she would not so readily have given up this custom, had it been forbidden by anyone she did not love so much as she did Ambrose. Because of his part in my spiritual growth, she was entirely devoted to him. And he appreciated talking with her on matters of faith. In her good works and fervent spiritual homage, she was constantly at church. When Ambrose saw me, he often abounded with her praise. He congratulated me that I had such a mother. He didn't know what a trial of a son she had in me, who expressed doubts about all things and declared that none could know the way to holy life.

I didn't yet pray earnestly that You would help me know You. My attention was wholly focused on education and debates. Ambrose himself seemed to be a happy man from the world's perspective. He was held in great honor. Only his celibacy appeared to be an unpleasant way to live.

Some things I couldn't understand because I hadn't experienced. I didn't understand the hope he bore within him or the struggles with temptations that lay behind his excellent life. I didn't understand where he got his comfort in time of trouble or what gracious joy he got as he bit into and chewed Your Bread in the hidden mouth of his spirit.

He did not know the ebb and flow of my emotions, or the danger I stood in on the edge of the precipice. I could not approach him as I would have preferred. His life was taken up with listening to and counseling a multitude of active people. He served them when they were weak. During what little time was not taken up with them, he was either taking a bare minimum of food and rest or he was absorbed with reading. As he read, his eye glided over the page, and his heart studied the meaning, and he rested his voice. His door was always open to all and anyone who wanted to see him had immediate access. When we visited him we often saw him absorbed in his reading. At such times we didn't want to intrude, so we sat quietly because we hated to leave his presence.

Friends

I had come to enjoy the study of the Law and the Prophets in Scripture. I no longer skimmed over the text with a skeptic's eye that found everything absurd. In my unbelief, I had looked down upon Your holy ones for believing ridiculous things that they did not even believe. Now I enjoyed hearing Ambrose preach and listened when he recommended some text as a rule to follow. The letter kills but the Spirit gives life. He drew aside the veil of misunderstanding, showing the spiritual significance in things that superficially had seemed to be nonsense or offended the intelligence. Whether his teaching was true, I wasn't sure. I refrained from expressing agreement with anything he taught, for fear of plunging headlong into another belief system.

The suspense was killing me. I wanted to be as sure of spiritual realities as I was that seven and three are ten. I was not so crazy a skeptic as to doubt that my mind could not comprehend numbers. I wanted all things to be as clearly true, whether material and open to the senses or spiritual. I couldn't see how to think through proofs except for physical, measurable things. If I had just put away my uncertainty, I would have found the vision aid to allow the eyes of the soul to see clearly. I could have found direction in Your truth, which always works and doesn't fail.

But someone who has been hurt by a bad physician is not so quick to trust a good one. I had learned that the health of my soul could not be healed by believing just anything. I was afraid I would come to believe more falsehoods. I refused the remedy and resisted Your therapy, even though You had prepared real medicines of faith. Your prescription had ministered to the diseases of the whole world with the power to heal.

Too weak to discern eternal truth through pure reasoning, we needed the authority of the holy Word. I considered that You would not have given such excelling authority to these writings in all the lands they reached if You had not wanted them to be sought out and believed. I had now heard many of the Scriptures explained that once had sounded strange and irrational. I now was willing to refer those things that still sounded absurd to the depths of mysteries. Scripture's authority appeared more eminent and worthy of acceptance in faith. While Scripture's clear meaning lay open to all, some of its most majestic mysteries lay ready to be uncovered by those who can grasp the profound. You stooped to all in the simplicity of the words and plain style. But You call forth the most intense application from those who will seek it. Everyone can come to Scripture and find a home and acceptance in its bosom. The breezes blowing through its narrow tunnels waft only a small number toward You. Yet far more are drawn than if it were not placed on such a high pedestal of authority, and multitudes more than if its words were not simple and intimate.

I thought about such things, and You were there with me.

I sighed, and You heard it.

I wavered, and You guided me on.

I wandered on through the broad avenue of the world's way, and You did not forsake me.

I yearned yet for honor, wealth, and marriage, and You mocked my pretensions.

The loss of these worldly dreams was difficult to bear. But the more gracious You became in leading me, the less attractive You made anything that was not Yourself. Look at my heart now, O Lord. Who would have thought that I would look back on these losses as part of my confession of You? Let my soul be bound only to You, now that You have freed it from that deadly snare that would have held me without escape. I felt wretched and You kept aggravating the wound until I would be willing to forsake all and belong to You. You are above all else in life, and until one is converted to You and healed by You, all things amount to nothing.

I was miserable, and how did You deal with me? You made me feel worse on the day when I was preparing to recite a laudatory essay for the Emperor.[1] In it I would utter many a lie, and the lies would be applauded by those who knew that I was lying. My heart was gasping from cares and hot with the fever of consuming worries.

Passing through one of the streets of Milan, I observed a poor beggar. Evidently he had a full belly that day, for he was laughing and joyful. I sighed and pointed him out to the friends around me. We were burdened with all the sorrows of our frenetic lives. We were goaded by our ambitions to keep up. I worked while dragging along the baggage of my own dissatisfaction, which was only feeling heavier. One day we hoped to arrive at the same state of joy that beggar was showing in front of us. He had the happiness we might never actually attain. He had obtained with a few coins he had begged from others the same state of satisfaction I was planning to gain by many a toilsome turning and winding.

It was all the joy of temporary comfort. What the beggar had gained was not the true joy, but it was just as real as what I was trying to get with my ambitious plans. Certainly he was happy, and I was anxious. He had no fears, while I was full of them. If the beggar had asked me whether I would prefer to be in his merry state or my own fearful one, I would have answered that I would rather be merry. On the other hand, if he asked whether I would rather be a beggar like him, I should say that I would choose to be myself, even though worn out with cares and fears. But was that poor judgment and was it the truth? Shouldn't I prefer to be like him? I had more knowledge than he, but no joy in all my pursuits. I was robbed of joy because I sought to please men by impressive deeds. I wasn't doing it to fulfill my role as a teacher, but simply to please.

This new understanding was a bone-cracking blow from the club of Your correction.

Get away from my soul, anyone who would say, "Certainly it makes a difference, where a man finds joy.

That beggar joyed in drunkenness.

You desired to find joy in glory."

What glory, Lord? Glory that is not found in You.

There was no true joy to be had and no true glory.

That turned my soul on its head yet more. The beggar that very night would begin to return to reality after his intoxication. I, on the other hand, would go to sleep in my stupor and wake up the same way, drunk with the desire to get ahead. I would go to sleep the next night and wake up the following day, and I would be no more in touch with reality.

How many nights would this go on? Only You, God, knew.

Yes, "it does make a difference where a man finds joy."

I know it does. The joy of a faithful hope lies very far from a scholar's egotism. That was why the beggar had moved beyond where I was. He was happier because he was thoroughly drenched in mirth, while I wasn't because I was hollow inside with cares. He had gotten precisely what he wanted in the wine. I listened to lies and sought empty, head-swelling praise.

I said this to my friends. I often looked at them and saw my own life mirrored. If I was like them, I decided, I was not doing well. That made me more depressed, which in turn made me feel twice as bad.

Good things were coming my way, but I was too downhearted to reach for them. And by the time I would have reached for the good thing, it had flown away.

We who were friends living together all bemoaned our lot. I mainly talked about these things in depth with Alypius and Nebridius.

Alypius was from my home town, born to noble parents. He was younger than I and had studied under me when I first lectured in Tagaste and then at Carthage. He loved me greatly, because I seemed kind and learned. I appreciated his desire to live a virtuous life, which seemed particularly strong in him for one so young.

It was not always so. At first he had been drawn into the whirlpool of watching time-wasting contests and games. Most Carthaginians avidly followed the madness of the circus.[2] But while he was caught up in the despicable life he didn't attend any of my classes, though I was instructing in rhetoric then at Carthage. The reason is that there were bad feelings between his father and me. I was aware of how caught up Alypius was in the circus. It distressed me that he seemed bent on throwing away his great abilities, if he hadn't already done so.

I was in no position to offer advice or to influence him to restrain his interest and thus bring him back to scholarship. I had neither friendship nor authority as his teacher to effect him. I then supposed that he disliked me as much as did his father. That was not the case, though, and he finally began to ignore his father's wishes. At first he only greeted me when we met on the street. Then he began showing up occasionally at my lectures. He would stay awhile and slip out.

I still did not confront him to keep him from ruining such a fine mind as he fell headlong into a thoughtless fanaticism for worthless pleasures. But You, O Lord, guide the paths of all You have created, and You didn't forget about him. You knew that one day he would be one of Your children, a priest who would conduct Your sacraments.

You wanted his reformation to be clearly from You, so I contributed to it without knowing how You were using me.

One day I sat in my customary seat in front of my students. He entered, greeted me, sat down, and applied his mind to the subject being taught. I happened to be explaining a passage describing the Circensian races.[3] To make the study more interesting and plain, I set up a sarcastic rhetorical banter about the games and the madness of those who were enthralled by them. You know, God, that I had no thought of the effect my jesting might have on Alypius and his addiction. But he took it completely to heart and assumed that I was doing it for his sake. Someone else might have felt offended that I was making fun of him. But this serious-minded young man saw reason to be offended only with himself. And he appreciated me for what I had done.

For You had said long ago in Your book, "Rebuke a wise man and he will love you."[4] I had not rebuked him, but You employ whatever means You wish, whether aware or unaware. You know the end for which You made my heart and tongue burning coals. It was a good purpose, to set ablaze a hopeful mind, curing what had been wasting away.

Let anyone who is unwilling to look into Your mercies remain silent.

Let him not give You praise.

I will look and then confess You from the center of my inmost being.

When he heard my speech, Alypius burst from that deep pit in which he had jumped. He shook off the blindness of these despicable amusements and asserted his self-control. All the pollution of the Circensian entertainment dropped away, and he never went back as long as he was in Carthage. After this, he again approached his father about becoming my student, and his father gave grudging permission.

At the time Alypius began attending my lectures again I was still quite involved with the Manichaean superstitions. He became caught up in it as well, desiring the ascetic lifestyle they made a great show of following. He assumed it was more genuine and sincere than it was. In fact, the asceticism had no real purpose, but it enticed a certain sort of sensitive soul. It ensnared many by promising a strong, wholesome morality, but it was just beguiling superficiality. Underneath, everything was smoke, a cheap imitation of life-changing values.

Alypius remained on the road to success in the world that his parents had convinced him to take. He left to go to Rome before I did. He studied law and incredibly again became swept up in the sporting events. Only now the shows included gladiator fights. He hated these despicable spectacles.

One day Alypius happened to meet a number of acquaintances and fellow-students who were coming from dinner. With the forceful horseplay of friends they pulled him along with them, strongly complaining and resisting, into the Amphitheater, during these cruel and deadly shows. He yelled, "You may be able to force my body into that place and set me on the seat, but you cannot force my mind or eyes to those shows. I will remain absent while present, and so overcome you all." They heard this but still forced him on, probably wanting to see if he could really avoid watching once he was inside.

When they had entered and taken their seats, the whole place seemed to be inflamed with the blood lust of this savage entertainment. But he kept his eyes shut and tried to shut off his mind from the evils. He wished he could also shut his ears. When one of the fighters fell a great cry went up from all the people. In the strong emotions of the moment, he was overcome with curiosity. Prepared to despise and remain aloof from whatever evil was before him, he opened his eyes and looked. His tender soul was stricken with a deeper wound than even the gladiator received in his body. He fell more miserably than did the one whose fall caused such a noise to be raised. The sounds that entered through his ears and the scene that unlocked his eyes struck and beat down his soul. He became bold to sin instead of more resolute. He was the weaker in that he presumed on his own strength instead of relying on You.

As soon as he saw that blood, he took a gulp of its savageness. Now he did not turn away. Instead he stared and drank in the frenzy. Now he was unaware even of how delighted he had become with that fight and how drunk with its violence. He was no longer the man who had entered the amphitheater but one of the throng. He was the true associate of the other young men who had brought him.

I need not say more about his actions. He watched, shouted, became impassioned, and was carried into the madness. He was impelled to return to the games with his friends, and to be there first and try to induce others to come. It was some time later that You used Your strong, merciful hand to pluck him from the lifestyle, teaching him to place his confidence in You instead of himself.

You did this when he was still studying under me at Carthage. He was in the public market and at mid-day, thinking through and memorizing, as scholars do, the answers he would give when called upon in class.

That was when You suddenly caught him up in an altercation and allowed that he should be identified as a thief. I believe You allowed him to be placed under arrest for no other reason but that one day he himself would be in a position of passing judgment on others. It was good that he learn from the beginning that it is not unusual for men to be unjustly condemned by a mob that is acting rashly, without thinking.

This young lawyer was simply pacing back and forth in thought in front of the judgment seat in the market, his books and stylus in hand.[5] Alypius did not notice that nearby, a thief was quietly using a hatchet to break through the lead grating on top of the silversmiths' shop. But someone did hear the man chopping away at the lead, and the silversmiths sent a guard to capture whoever was found on the roof. The thief heard them and ran off, leaving his hatchet behind so he wouldn't be caught with it. Alypius had not seen the man sneak in, but he did notice him leaving and took note of the speed of his departure. Curious to know what was going on, he entered the place where the thief had been and found the hatchet. So the guards found him alone with the hatchet in his hand that had made all the noise. They immediately seized him and hauled him away. Soon all the merchants of the market gathered at news that a notorious thief had been caught, and he was led away to face the magistrate.

Lord, You allowed the lesson to teach Alypius to proceed this far before You showed the rest that he was innocent, although You alone knew it. As he was being led either to prison or to punishment, the chief architect, who was in charge of all the public buildings of the city, met them. The merchants were happy to see the official since he sometimes suspected them of stealing the goods that were lost in the market. They wanted to show him who had been committing these thefts.

Fortunately, the man had frequently seen Alypius in the home of a senator where they both visited socially. He extricated Alypius, took him aside, and asked what had caused this calamity. He listened to the explanation and told all the crowd, who were still in an uproar and making many threats, to follow him. They reached the house of the young man who really was the culprit. A young servant boy came to the door who didn't understand that he wasn't supposed to be perfectly honest with all of these people, nor that any harm might come to his master. The boy had accompanied his master to the market and was seen and described by Alypius and recognized by the architect. The architect showed the hatchet to the boy and asked if he knew to whom it belonged.

"It is ours," he said. Through further questions the entire story was worked out. Thus suspicion was transferred to that house, and the mob was ashamed for jumping to conclusions and insulting Alypius.

One day he would become a dispenser of Your Word, and an examiner of many causes in Your Church, and that day he went away better taught and prepared for the task.

After I found him at Rome, he remained strongly attached to me. Alypius went with me to Milan, both because he wanted to remain with me and so that he might practice the law, although he had studied more to please his parents than himself. Three times in Milan he sat as an arbiter in the courts and earned a reputation for being above corruption that was a public wonder. For his part, he was just as amazed that others so preferred gaining wealth to honesty.

So it was not by a covetous nature that he was tempted but by being provoked by fear. At Rome he was arbiter to the Count of the Italian Treasury.[6] There was at that time a very powerful senator to whom many owed favors and others feared. He usually was given any consideration he wished, even if it was against the law. Alypius refused a request from this senator and then turned down the bribe that was promised. He held out when threats were made. This just was not done, and all who knew about his stand wondered at this uncommon character that did not care to make a powerful friend and did not fear the enmity of the great man. His courage was the greater because this man was famous for doing great good for his friends and doing great evil in revenge.

The situation was worse because the judge over Alypius did not want to openly offend the senator, so he made certain that Alypius alone was blamed. The judge told representatives of the senator that he was willing to accede to their request, but Alypius would not allow him to do it. There was truth here, for if the judge had done it, Alypius would have stood against him.

In the end the senator made life so difficult that Alypius almost gave in, for he could not even afford to purchase copied books for his studies without paying exorbitant prices. However, after some deliberation he decided to take the higher path, regarding fairness more highly than the power he could have gained had he given in.

These are small matters, but when someone is faithful in little, he is faithful also in much. Nor will the promises in Your truth ever be found to be worthless. Unless someone is faithful in handling the temptations of wealth, who will commit to him true riches? And those unfaithful with another's life will not be given real authority over their own. Through this experience Alypius kept close to me and came to me when he was wavering that he might know which way to go.

Another student, named Nebridius, left his native country near Carthage and journeyed from Carthage to come to Milan because he wanted to study with me. He left behind a magnificent home and lands and his mother, who was instructed not to follow him. He sought to join me in an ardent search for truth and wisdom. Like me he sighed; like me he wavered, a zealous seeker after true life, and a most acute analyst of the most difficult questions.

Thus we became a household of three indigents who lifted mouths to be fed, sighing their wants to one another, and waiting upon You to give them their food at the proper time.[7] And in all the sorrows of our worldly lives through which Your mercy led us, we looked to see Your purposes for suffering and saw only darkness. We averted our eyes and groaned, "How long shall these things be?" We often made such complaints and stuck with seeking the answers, since no certain responses had yet dawned on us. We looked for something that we forsaken souls might embrace.

A number of those in our circle of friends were similarly dissatisfied with the turbulence and turmoil of human affairs. We talked together and debated and almost resolved to live apart from the business and the bustle of humanity. We considered how this might be accomplished. Each of us would gather all the resources we could and bring them together to make a single joint household. Staying true to our friendship for each other, nothing should belong to any one of us. But all the possessions that we jointly could gather would belong to each, and each thing to all.

We considered that about ten persons might be the ideal number for this society. Some of those among us were very rich, especially Romanianus,[8] who came from my home town and I had known from childhood. He was a very close friend. He had struggled to learn to keep track of the intricacies of his family affairs and in particular a most difficult court case concerning his estate, and he was the most ardent supporter of our project. His vote carried the most weight, because he had far more to share than any of the rest of us.

We decided that two annual officers should provide all necessary purchases, not bothering the rest with worldly matters. The plan fell to pieces in our hands, however, when we realized that some of us were married and others planned to marry. We could not decide how to make this society fit around wives. So the plan was utterly dashed and cast aside. We had many ideas, but Your counsel stands forever. With sighs and groans, we went out to make our way through the broad, beaten paths of the world. Your plan put ours to shame, and Your purposes would provide for us. You would open Your hand and fill our souls with blessing.

Notes

1. Perhaps Valentinian the Younger, whose court, according to Possidius, was at Milan when Augustine was professor of rhetoric there. Augustine

writes in a letter that he "recited on the first of January a panegyric to Bauto the consul as required by his then profession of rhetoric."

2. Carthage is known to have had a circus, but the site was later dismantled, and historians had only Augustine's word about the fanaticism for chariot racing and other circus games. Then in 1992 an excavation team working under archaeologist Naomi Norman at a large cemetery on the road leading to the circus, unearthed a magnificent marble statue of a charioteer. Such a memorial on a mausoleum is almost without precedent. Charioteers could become extremely wealthy, but almost all were former slaves, and successful racers were usually treated with disdain and tried to forget their time in the games. To erect such an expensive funerary statue of a charioteer indicates that they had a much higher social status in Carthage than elsewhere in the Empire.

3. Circensian games included Greek-style athletic contests and chariot and foot races. The Circus Maximus in Rome made a great spectacle of such games. The Circensian games were more modest affairs held in the provinces, patterned after those of the Circus Maximus.

4. Proverbs 9:8b.

5. A typical Roman marketplace (*agora*) had a raised platform with a stone seat on it in which public officials sat to convene meetings or convene court proceedings. This was the *bema*.

6. The Lord High Treasurer of the Western Empire was called *Comes Sacrarum largitionum*. He had six other treasurers in so many provinces under him, whereof he of Italy was one.

7. Cf. Psalm 104:27.

8. Romanianus was a relation of Alypius, of a talent which astonished Augustine himself. He "had been always surrounded by affluence and had been snatched by what are thought adverse circumstances from the absorbing whirlpools of life." Augustine frequently mentions his great wealth and this vexing legal suit that harassed him and clouded his mind. He was so distracted by life that his talents went almost undeveloped. He showed great kindness to Augustine by giving him a place in his home and supporting him when Augustine was a student. Augustine also speaks of the spiritual growth that Romanianus had encouraged in him.

The Way of Perfection

I came to the point where I conceived of You as existing in the physical reality of space. I still preferred to believe that You were incorruptible, invulnerable, and unchangeable, as opposed to being corruptible, vulnerable, and variable. I considered whether Your being was infused into the world, or diffused infinitely through the universe. The problem was that I could not imagine a being that transcended material reality might be real. If You were outside of everything, I reasoned that You were altogether nothing. If a body could be taken out of a void, so that the void was truly empty of material earth, water, air, or star matter, would not such a place be no more than a spacious nothing?

These mental wanderings were thick-headed and not clear even to myself. Whatever did not have measurable bulk, whatever could not be diffused, whatever could not contract or expand to some sort of dimensions—such things, I thought, must be altogether nothing. My faith was no larger than what my eyes could see. It never occurred to me that the very mental processes I used to reason such things were real enough to do wondrous things and form marvelous images, yet it did not have form of the sort I was demanding that my God fit.

I also tried to conceive of You, Life of my life, as vast, taking up infinite space. I imagined Your bulk in some sense penetrating the whole mass of the universe and beyond. I thought how you might extend through immeasurable boundless spaces, so that the earth should have You, the heavens have You, all things have You and be bounded in You and You bounded nowhere. I reasoned that You were like the body of this air that lies above the earth. The air doesn't stop sunlight from passing through. The light penetrates air, not by bursting or cutting through it but by filling it wholly. So I imagined that Your body was such that heaven, air, sea, and earth could fill you as light fills sky. In such a universe, the greatest and the smallest objects should admit Your presence by a secret inspiration, within and without, directing all things You created.

That was my guess, since I was unable to consider an alternative. But my idea was false. If it were true that all things were full of You, larger things would contain more of you than things of smaller size, the elephant more than a sparrow. Thus You would make the numerous pieces of Yourself present in numerous pieces of the world. You would be fragmented, large pieces and small. That is how You are. But at that time You had not enlightened my darkness.

❧

You were my Guide, and You helped me return to viewing reality through the eyes of my soul, such as I had, instead of placing the eyes of my mind above the eyes of my soul. Through spiritual eyes I was better able to see the Light Unchangeable. This is no ordinary light of the sort that all people can see. It is not even a superbly bright light that fills space with luminescence. No, this Light was not a natural light. It was far different from anything in natural human experience.

This Light was not separate from my mind, as oil naturally separates and rises above water. It was not different from my self-awareness as the sky rises apart from the earth.

But this Light did stand above my soul, because the Light made me;

I stood below the Light, because I was made by it.

He that knows the truth knows what that Light is.

And he that knows truth knows eternity.

And he that knows love knows truth.

O Truth who is Eternity!

O Love who is Truth!

O Eternity who is Love!

You are my God. To You do I sigh night and day.

When I first knew You, You raised my perspective so that I could better see. As yet, I could not look out from this height. But You did beat back the dark shadows from my weak eyes with Your strong, streaming beams of illumination. In the glare, I trembled with love and awe, and I perceived that I was far off from You. I was living in a region foreign to You, and I heard Your voice from a distant height:

"I am the food of grown men. Grow up. Then you will feed upon Me. What you eat of Me will not change Me, as food changes when taken into your body. Rather, eat the food of My flesh, and you will be changed until you are like Me."

I know how You correct the one who sins. You made my soul waste away like a spider. When I asked "Is truth therefore nothing because it is not diffused through space—finite or infinite?" You answered loudly from afar, "Yes, truly, I am who I am."

I heard, as the heart hears, nor did You allow me room for doubt. I would rather doubt that I live than that there is no absolute Truth. It can be clearly seen and understood in the things that are made.[1]

As I listened to Your high voice, I beheld other things that are below You. I saw that some things exist because they are from You. Other things do not exist because they did not originate in You. But only One truly exists and remains unchangeably existing. It is then good for me to hold fast unto God, for if I remain not in Him, I cannot live in myself. But since He remains steadfast, He is able to renew all things.

You are the Lord my God, who stands in no need of my goodness in order for You to exist.

❧

It is amazing that I now love You, and not some fantasy version of You. Yet I did not press on to enjoy my God. My soul was carried heavenward to You by Your beauty, yet it was pushed back from You by my own weight. I sank, groaning, into inferior things. This weight was carnal custom. Yet at my lowest, a remembrance of You lived in me. Nor did I doubt at all that there was One to whom I might cling. I was simply not yet prepared to cling to You.

The body that is corrupted presses down the soul. The earthly tabernacle weighs down the mind that muses upon many things. That was my situation. Your invisible works from the creation of the world are clearly seen, being understood by the things that are made, even Your eternal power and Godhead.[2]

I examined my thoughts, why it was that I admired the natural beauty of things in the heavens and on earth. What standard helped me accurately judge the changing things of creation and declare, "This is reasonable; that is not"? What was it that made me judge, because I obviously did judge? I had found an unchangeable eternal truth that existed apart from my changeable mind. By degrees, I passed from my awareness of external bodies through the bodily senses to the soul. What I learned from the senses I analyzed with my inward faculties, which can internalize facts about external things. Animals can do that much. The reasoning faculty receives what is learned from the senses and makes judgments. I found reason itself to be in me a variable thing.

But my understanding was able to raise itself to a higher understanding when it pulled back from thoughts that originate in habit. Withdrawing from the troops of contradictory chimera thoughts, my mind can seek a clearer light and be enlightened without being filled with doubt. The mind cries that the unchangeable is to be preferred over the changeable. It knows that an unchangeable does exist. If it did not know, it would not have been so dissatisfied with the changeable.

And thus with the flash of one trembling glance, my mind arrived at "That Which Is." In that moment of clarity, I saw Your invisible things that can be discerned from seeing what You have made. I could not yet fix my gaze on those things, for my fallen self struck back. I fell back into old habits of thought, but from that vision of truth I carried away a memory and a longing to see more. I had caught a whiff of truth, but I was not yet able to feed on it.

I continued to look for a way to obtain sufficient strength to enjoy You, but I did not find the power until I embraced Jesus Christ as Mediator between God and humanity. It is Jesus who is over all, God eternally blessed.[3] It is He who called to me, "I am the way and the truth and the life."[4] Jesus mingled that food that I was unable to receive with human flesh. For the Word became flesh, that Your wisdom, whereby You created all things, might provide milk for our infant state.

I did not yet hold to my Lord Jesus Christ. I had been humbled, but I could not yet find my way to the Humble. Nor could I yet discern what lessons this lowly teacher would give. Your word, the eternal Truth, far above the higher parts of Your Creation, raises up the meek. He came into this lower world to build for Himself a lowly habitation of human clay. He was abased to find such as would be subdued and bring them over to Himself. He heals their swelling, and nurtures their love so that they might go no farther in self-confidence. Rather He seeks those who will become weak, seeing before their feet the Divinity who became weak by taking our coats of skin. He was wearied that the weary might cast themselves down upon Him and be lifted up in His rising.

But I thought otherwise. I conceived of my Lord Christ as a man of excellent wisdom, greater than that of all other men. He was wonderfully born of a Virgin. He seemed to have conformed Himself to the Divine care for us until He attained great eminence of authority. He lived as an example of despising temporal things in order to obtain immortality.

But I could not even imagine what mystery lay behind the words "The Word became flesh. . . ." I kept to the bare essentials of how He was described in writings. I knew that

He ate and drank, slept, walked, rejoiced in spirit, and was sorrowful. I knew He taught that flesh does not mingle with Your Word. Flesh attaches to humanity, alongside soul and mind. Anyone who grasps the unchangeable nature of Your Word figures this out. I knew that much and was certain of it. By direction of my will, I may move the limbs of my body and then stop. I can be moved in body and inner self by some love and then stop the emotion. I can speak wise sayings through signs that communicate with other humans, and then keep silent. The flesh belongs to soul and mind, and it is subject to change.

But if Scripture were false in saying that it was the Word that became flesh, then all Scripture might be falsified. Then no authoritative source would speak of saving faith for humankind. Now I know that these things are true. Then I only knew truly that in Christ there was a complete man. I understood that Christ was more than just the body of a man. His body was attached to a sensitive soul and a rational mind. He was very man, not just an idealized form of Truth. There was great excellence in His human nature and a more perfect participation of wisdom than I judged could be found in all others.

Notes

1. Cf. Romans 1:19–20.
2. Cf. Romans 1:20.
3. Cf. 1 Timothy 2:5.
4. John 14:6.

Simplicianus

To Simplicianus then I went, the spiritual father of the bishop Ambrose, whom Ambrose truly loved as a father. To him I described the intellectual maze in which I had been wandering. I mentioned that I had read certain books of the Platonists, which had been translated into Latin by Victorinus, a sometime rhetoric professor of Rome. I had heard that this Victorinus had died a Christian. Simplicianus expressed pleasure that I had not fallen upon the writings of other philosophers who are full of fallacy and deceit as they deal with elemental worldly thinking. The thinking of Platonists, however, can lead in the end to God, and His Word. Their thoughts encourage one toward the humility of Christ, which is hidden from the wise and revealed to little ones.

While he had lived in Rome, Simplicianus had been a close friend to Victorinus. I will not conceal the story he related, for it contains great praise of Your grace, which should be confessed to You. That aged man was most learned and skilled in the liberal sciences, and had read and analyzed many works of the philosophers. He had taught many noble senators, who had recognized his excellent work with a high honor in the eyes of the world. Victorinus deserved and had been accorded a statue in the Roman Forum. Until that time he had been a worshiper of idols and a participant in the unholy rites popular among most of Rome's nobility. He had inspired people with the love of Anubis, the barking deity, and other monstrous gods of every sort who fought against Neptune, Venus, and Minerva. Rome had conquered the lands of these gods and now adored them.

The aged Victorinus had long defended the gods with thundering eloquence, but suddenly he was not ashamed to be the child of Your Christ, the newborn baby at Your fountain. He submitted his neck to the yoke of humility, and bowed his head to the reproach of the cross.

O Lord, who has tore the heavens and came down,[1] Lord who touched the mountains and they did smoke,[2] by what means did You convey Yourself into that man's heart? Victorinus read the holy Scripture, according to Simplicianus, and searched out and studied all the Christian writings that were available. Privately as friend to friend, he told Simplicianus, "Understand that I am already a Christian."

Simplicianus answered, "I will not believe it, nor will I rank you among Christians, unless I see you in the Church of Christ."

The other, in jest, replied, "Do walls then make Christians?" He frequently made this comment that he was already a Christian, and Simplicianus challenged him each time with the same answer. And each time, the man defended his secret confession with the same quip about "walls." For Victorinus was afraid of offending his proud, demon-worshiping friends. They lived in the heights of Babylonian dignity, stately as cedars of Lebanon that the Lord had not yet broken down. In his high position, Victorinus supposed that the weight of enmity would fall upon him if he openly rejected the gods.

But he kept reading and earnestly thinking, and finally he gathered courage, for he more feared to be denied by Christ before the holy angels because he now was afraid to confess Christ before men. He realized that he was guilty of a serious offense. He was ashamed to partake of the sacraments in submission to Your Word, yet he had not been ashamed of taking part in the sacrilegious rites of haughty demons, whose pride he had imitated and whose rites he had adopted. He boldly faced up to his own vanity, and his shame towards the truth.

Simplicianus told me that Victorinus suddenly and unexpectedly said to him, "Let us go to the church. I wish to be made a Christian." Overflowing with joy, he went with him. Victorinus was admitted to the first sacrament[3] and became a catechumen. Not long after he further gave in his name, that he might be reborn in baptism.[4] Rome wondered. The Church rejoiced. The proud saw and were angry. They gnashed their teeth, and melted away from his association. But by this time the Lord God was the only hope of Your servant, and he had stopped caring about their vain lives and mad lies.

At Rome, catechumens who are about to approach the sacrament of Your grace stand on an elevated platform before all the church and speak from memory the words of confession.[5] When the hour had finally come for Victorianus to make full profession of faith, the church presbyters[6] offered him the option of making his profession privately. This was allowed for those who were afraid to speak before the public assembly. But he chose rather to profess his salvation in the presence of the holy multitude. For he had publicly taught rhetoric, which was far less important than his profession of salvation. So when pronouncing Your word, he would not feel dread before Your meek flock if he had not feared to deliver his own words before the mad multitude.

When this well-recognized public figure went up to make his profession, all knew him and whispered his name to each other, sharing in this special moment. Was there anyone there who did not know who this was? A low murmur of recognition passed though all the mouths of the rejoicing multitude.

Victorinus! Victorinus! There was a sudden burst of rapture when they saw him.

Then a hush fell over the body so that they might hear him.

He pronounced the true faith with an excellent boldness, and all wished to draw him into their very heart. Indeed, by their love and joy, they did take him to themselves. Such were the hands extended to draw him into the fellowship.

I wondered as I heard the story, oh God of goodness, what takes place in us that we so rejoice at the salvation of someone no one expected would come, or someone who has been freed from a life of particular peril in godlessness. Why should the joy be greater than for one who had always been expected to come to Christ, or whose life was less in danger?

Perhaps there is reason for this. You also, as merciful Father, rejoice over one penitent more than over ninety-nine just persons who need no repentance. We hear of Your joyfulness, comparable to the joy when a sheep that has strayed is brought back upon the Shepherd's shoulder.[7] The valuable coin is restored to Your treasury, and we hear how the neighbors rejoiced with the woman who found such a lost coin.[8] At such times, the joy of the solemn occasion in Your house forces all to tears. It is as when we read of the younger son who was dead, and lived again, who had been lost and was found.

For You rejoice in us, and in Your holy angels, holy in sanctified love.

You are ever the same.

All things in life do not last, nor are they the same forever.

But You always know in the same way.

What then takes place in the soul? It is more delightful to find or recover something beloved that has been lost than if it had been at hand? Yes, that is a witness to an eternal verity. Our experience is full of such witnesses. They cry out, "This is like the hidden reality."

The conquering commander triumphs.

He would not have conquered, unless he had fought.

The more peril in the battle, the sweeter his victory.

The storm tosses the sailors, threatening shipwreck.

All are terrified as death looms.

Then sky and sea grow calm.

The sailors feel exceeding joy, to the measure of their fear.

A friend is sick, so weak that his pulse grows faint.

All who long for his recovery are sick with him in worry.

Then he survives.

He cannot yet walk with his former strength.

But the joy is greater than if he had always walked sound and strong.

Yes, there are inexpressible pleasures in life that must be acquired through difficulties, whether the hard times fall upon us out of nowhere against our wills, or whether they are the result of chosen paths of pleasure-seeking trouble. Eating and drinking have no special pleasure, unless these follow the pinch of hunger and thirst. Men who are given to drink may eat salty meat to produce the discomfort of heat and thirst. Then they quench their thirst with a drink and feel greater enjoyment. It is also the custom, that the betrothed bride is not immediately given to the bridegroom. This adds to his longing, so that when he is a husband he will not hold cheap the one he has sighed for.

The higher transport is ushered in by the deeper pain. This law holds whether in foul and accursed enchantment or in a delight that is appropriate and lawful. It holds in relationships of purest friendship. It holds in relation to the one who has been dead, and lives again, who was lost and is found.

What means this, O Lord my God? Whereas You have everlastingly joy in Yourself, and You are surrounded forever by rejoicing in You. What is the ultimate purpose of ebb and flow, alternate displeasure and reconciliation? Is this the allotted measure? Is this part of the plan you have established for us? From the highest heavens to the lowest earth, from the beginning of the world to the end of ages, from angel to worm, from first motion to last, You have given each thing its place and time. You have made good to come from its kind.

Woe is me! How high are You in the highest. How deep are Your deepest reasonings. You never depart, and we scarcely return to You.

Up, Lord, then; stir us up.

Recall us; kindle and draw us.

Inflame and grow sweet to us.

Let us now love. Let us run.

Do not many come to You from out of a deeper hell of blindness than that of Victorinus? You let them approach and be enlightened. You ignite that light that they receive and give them the power to become Your sons.

Notes

1. Cf. Isaiah 64:1–2.
2. Cf. Psalm 104:31–32.
3. The Lord's Supper. Baptism might be put off until after an extended period of instruction. Traditionally, baptisms were only performed on the Sunday marking the Resurrection. A catechumen who confessed Christ might be accepted provisionally to partake of the Lord's Supper and be regarded as part of the body for some time before he or she was baptized. This seems to have been the case with Victorinus.
4. Adults were given a new "Christian" name at baptism, since the sacrament marked their new birth and new identity in Christ.
5. Churches developed individual baptismal confessions, which were memorized during the time of catechumen instruction and recited before administration of the sacrament of baptism. The most enduring baptismal confession was that of the Roman church, which was first recorded in about the year 116. This confession was refined in small ways over the centuries but by about 700 reached the form in which it still is used in worship liturgy. It is now most often identified as the Apostle's Creed.
6. Or "elders," lay leaders as well as pastors who were in charge of the worship and spiritual welfare of the people.
7. Cf. Luke 15:4–6.
8. Cf. Luke 15:8–9.

The Death of Monnica

Receive my confessions and thanksgiving, O my God, for innumerable things whereof I am silent.

But I will not omit what my soul would offer concerning Your handmaid. She was the one who brought me forth in the flesh, that I might be born to this temporal light, and who gave birth to my heart, that I might be born to Light eternal.[1] I would not speak of her gifts, though, but the gifts that You placed in her. She neither made nor educated herself. You created her. Her father and mother did not know what a one should come from them. The scepter of Your Christ taught her in Your fear, the discipline of Your only Son in a Christian house and membership in Your Church.

For her good discipline, she did not so much commend her mother's example. She remembered rather a certain worn out maid-servant who had carried my mother's father when he was a child, as little ones were carried on the backs of elder girls. For that reason, and for her great age and wisdom, she was well respected by the heads of that Christian family. She was given charge of her master's daughters. She raised them with diligence, restraining them earnestly when necessary with a holy severity. She taught them with grave discretion. Except at those set times when they were given proper meals at their parents' table, she would not allow them even a drink, although parched with thirst. She did this to prevent an evil custom, explaining with the wholesome advice, "You drink water now, because you do not have access to wine. When you come to be married and are mistresses of cellars and cupboards, you will scorn water for other drinks if you have the habit of always quenching your thirst." By this method of instruction and the authority she had, she kept them from the greediness of childhood, and molded even their thirst to an excellent moderation, so they should be able to discipline themselves about what they should and should not have.

Despite this training, as Your handmaid admitted to me later, she developed a love of wine. The custom of the family was that she, who was thought a sober maiden, should be sent by her parents to draw wine from the storage vat for meals. While holding the vessel under the opening, before she poured the wine into the flagon, she sipped a little with the tip of her lips. Her conscience allowed no more. She sampled, not out of a desire for drink, but out of the exuberance of youth. Youthful revels can boil over unless the spirit is kept in check by the gravity of elders. So little was added to little each day. Whoever fails to watch small things will fall by such little upon little. She almost fell into a habit of greedily drinking her little cup to the brim of wine.

What had become of that discreet old woman and her earnest correction? Would anything avail against the secret disease, if Your healing hand did not watch over us? Father, mother, and governors were not there, but You who created and calls were there. You use those who are set over us to begin working toward the salvation of our souls.

What did You then, O my God? How did You cure her? How did You bring healing to her? You used the sharp-tongued taunt of another soul as a lancet out of Your secret kit. With a touch You lanced the boil and drained all that foul stuff. A maid-servant who had sometimes been in the cellar came to exchange words of anger with her little mistress. While they were alone, the girl taunted her about this fault. The most bitter insult the servant could think of was to call her a drunk. That ridicule stung, as she saw the evil of her fault, and she instantly condemned and forsook the habit.

As flattering friends pervert, so reproachful enemies mostly correct. Yet You punish evil intent, even if You used what was done for good. The servant girl in her anger wanted to hurt her young mistress, not to amend her. She made the hurtful remark in private, either because that was simply where the quarrel developed or because the girl was afraid she would be in trouble for not telling about the drinking habit earlier. But You, Lord, Governor of all in heaven and earth, turn the deepest currents to Your purposes. You rule over turbulence of the tide of times, so that their very unhealthiness can heal. This is clearly Your doing, lest anyone should say that he had obtained a good outcome in his own strength. The observer must admit that healing is from You, even when others become Your servants, lest any could think that a changed soul can be obtained by human words.

Brought up modestly and soberly, she was made subject by You to her parents, more than by her parents to You. When she was of marriageable age, she was given to a husband and served him as her lord. She did her best to win him unto You, speaking about You to him through her speech, her amiable reverence, and other traits that her husband admired. She so endured his offenses of infidelity and did not quarrel with her husband about them.

For she looked for Your mercy to come to him, that he might become chaste through belief in You. Besides his unfaithfulness, he was a man of great passions, both in his affection and in his explosive temper: She had learned to submit to her husband in word and deed, even when he became angry. Only after his anger subsided, when he was able to listen, did she explain and defend actions that he had hastily taken offense at.

Other wives of milder husbands openly showed resentment on their faces and would complain to the family about their husbands' lives. When she heard such complaints, she would tell them to hold their tongues, giving serious advice in the humorous quip that, from the time they heard the marriage vows, they should regard their marriage contract as a servant's contract of indenture. Remembering that they were servants, they should not set themselves against their lords.

Those who understood what a difficult husband she endured marveled that she never spread reports of ill treatment, even if Patricius had beaten her or had been unfair in a domestic difference between them. In confidence she was asked why she put up with such faults. This is when she made the statement about an indentured servant. Those wives who accepted her counsel found the good, and returned thanks. Some who did not understand or follow her advice suffered for it.

At first her mother-in-law listened to whisperings of evil servants and angrily blamed her for the problems of her marriage. Eventually the mother-in-law's anger was overcome by what she saw for herself, including Monnica's persevering endurance and meekness. She discovered who was telling the stories about her daughter-in-law and told her son to punish those who had tried to destroy their relationship. Complying with his mother and to keep order and harmony in his family, he corrected those who had spread lies with a whip. His mother promised that the same would be done to anyone else who should try to win favor with her by speaking ill of her daughter-in-law to her. Thereafter, none ventured to do so, and the two women lived together with a remarkably sweet mutual friendship.

You also bestowed upon Your good handmaid, in whose womb You created me, O merciful God, the gift of peacemaking between others who were in discord. She listened to both sides of a bitter dispute, the result of swelling, undigested bitterness when it breaks into the open, when enmity breathes out its crudities in sour discourses to a present friend against an absent enemy. She never would disclose anything that one side would say about the other unless she could use it to encourage reconciliation.

This discretion might appear to me to be an obvious good. However, to my grief I have known numerous persons who were trapped in some horrible and spreading contagion of sin. Such people not only disclose to persons mutually hurtful things said about them in anger, but they add things that were not even spoken. It seems only humane and reasonable to avoid fomenting or increasing ill will by adding provocative words, unless one study withal by good words how to quench the fire. She learned peacemaking from You, her most inward Instructor, in the school of the heart.

In the end, toward the end of his earthly life, this worthy wife did gain her own husband for You. Never did she again have the problems with him that she had suffered before he became a believer. She was also the servant of Your servants. Those of Your servants who knew her had reason to give to You much praise and honor and love because of her. They witnessed in her the fruits of Your holy fellowship with her and perceived Your presence in her heart. For she had been the wife of one man, had honored her parents, had governed her house piously, and was well reported of for good works. She had brought up children after travailing in birth, and she travailed when she saw them swerving from You. Lastly, she took care of all of us who are Your servants, O Lord (for You allow us to speak of such things), as though she had been mother of us all. As long as she lived, she served us who lived united in the grace of Your baptism. It was as though she was a daughter to us all.

As the day of her departure from this life approached, a day You well knew though we did not, it came to pass that she and I stood alone, leaning in a certain window that looked into the garden of the house where we resided at Ostia. I believe You ordered this time in Your secret ways, where we were removed from the din of men. We were resting after a long voyage.

We talked together alone, very sweetly, forgetting those things of the past and reaching toward those things which were before.[2] We were inquiring between ourselves in the presence of the Truth that You are, what sort of eternal life the saints were to have. Such things eye has not seen, nor ear heard, nor has the full answer entered into the heart.[3] But yet we gasped with the mouth of

139

our heart, after those heavenly streams of Your fountain, the fountain of life, which is with You. We wanted to be enlightened as much as we could comprehend, so that we might better meditate upon so high a mystery.

And when our conversation reached that point, the very highest delight of the earthly senses, in the very purest material light, was not worth comparing to the sweetness of that life. We saw that this life is not worthy even of mention. We raised up ourselves with a more glowing affection towards the creation realities. By degrees we passed over all material being, to the very heavens where the sun, moon, and stars shine upon the earth. We soared higher yet in our inward musings, and considered and admired all of Your works.

We came to the wonder of our own minds, and went beyond them, that we might arrive at that region of never-failing plenty.

There You feed Israel forever with the food of truth.

There life is that Wisdom by whom all these things are made, the "have been" and the "shall be" things.

There is the Wisdom that is not made, but is, as she has been, and shall ever be.

States of "have been," and "hereafter will be," are not in her.

This Wisdom just "is," for she is eternal.

"Have been" and "will hereafter be" are not eternal.

And while we were considering eternal Wisdom and panting after her, we slightly touched on Wisdom with the whole effort of our heart. The wonder brought a sigh, and there we left bound the first fruits of the Spirit; and returned to consider the vocal expressions of our mouth, for the word spoken has both a beginning and an end.[4]

And what is like unto Your Word, our Lord, who endures in Himself without becoming old, and who makes all things new?[5]

We were saying then:

If to any the tumult of the flesh were hushed,

hushed the images of earth, and waters, and air,

hushed the poles of heaven.

hushed the very soul,

hushed all dreams and imaginary revelations,

hushed every tongue and sign, and whatsoever exists only in transition—in that silence, if any could hear, all of these would say, "We made not ourselves, but He made us that abides forever."

Having said this, they too should be silent, having opened our ears to Him who made them. Then He alone would speak, not by them, but by Himself, that we may hear His Word. His voice would not be spoken through any tongue of flesh, nor angel's voice, nor sound of thunder, nor in the dark riddle of a similitude. Rather we might hear the One whom in these things we love, might hear His very Self without these (as we two now strained ourselves, and in swift thought touched on that Eternal Wisdom, which abides over all).

Could this sight be continued, and all other, lesser and unlike visions cease, and this one ravish, and absorb, and wrap up its beholder amid these inward joys, life might be forever like that one moment of understanding which now we sighed after.

Isn't this the final meaning of "Come and share your master's happiness"?[6]

And when shall that be?

When we shall all rise again, though we shall not all be changed?[7]

I said such things, if not in this exact manner and wording. Lord, You know that as we spoke that day of these things, the delights of the world became contemptible to us. My mother said, "Son, for mine part, I have no further delight in anything in this life. What I am to do and why I am here any longer, I do not know. My hopes in this world are accomplished. There was one thing that I longed to see while I lived, and that was for you to be a catholic Christian. My God has been more than generous in giving this to me, for I have seen you despise earthly happiness to become His servant. So now what am I doing here?"

I don't remember the answer I gave. It was not much more than five days later that she fell sick of a fever. After being sick one day, she fell unconscious, and for a while withdrew from all visible things. We hastened around her, but she regained consciousness, looked at my brother and me as we stood by, and inquired, "Where was I?"[8] And then looking fixedly on us in our surprised grief, she added, "Here you will bury your mother."

I held my peace and refrained from weeping, but my brother said something about his wish that it would be better if she died in her homeland, rather than this strange place. Her anxious look of reproach stopped him, for it bothered her that he considered such things important. "Hear what he says," she said to me. Soon she spoke to us both: "Lay this body anywhere. Do not be in any way concerned about it. I ask only that you remember me at the Lord's altar, wherever you are." After saying this as well as she could, she fell silent, worn out as she became more ill.

Considering the gifts, unseen God, that You instill in the hearts of Your faithful ones, from which wondrous fruits do spring, I rejoiced and gave thanks. I remembered that at one time she had been most anxious in caring for her place of burial, which she had prepared for herself by the body of her husband. Since they had lived in great harmony together, she also wished to have this addition to that happiness. So little can the human mind embrace eternal things that she had wanted it remembered among men that after her pilgrimage beyond the seas, what was earthly of this united pair was united beneath the same earth.

I did not know that her heart had begun to let go of this emptiness through the fullness of Your goodness. I rejoiced to delight in what she had made known to me. Certainly as we talked by the window, she had expressed no particular desire to die in her own country as she asked, "What am I still doing here?" I heard afterwards that when we were at Ostia, she had spoken to some of my friends with a mother's confidence about her contempt for this life, and the blessing of death. They expressed surprise at such courage as You had given to a woman and asked whether she feared to leave her body so far from her own city.

She replied, "Nothing is far to God. Should I fear that at the end of the world He will not know where to raise me up?"

On the ninth day of her sickness, in the fifty-sixth year of her life, and the thirty-third year of mine, that righteous and holy soul was freed from the body. Despite everything, when I closed her eyes I felt a mighty sorrow. It overflowed in emotion. My eyes answered the violent command of my emotions to fill with enough water to drink a fountain completely dry. I was tormented by conflicts. When she breathed her last, the boy Adeodatus burst out into a loud lament. Then he was stopped by us all and remained silent. I felt the same childish feeling well up in my heart. My heart's youthful cry wanted an outlet in crying, but I stopped myself and remained silent. We did not think it appropriate to conduct this funeral with tearful lament and groaning. This is the usual custom for expressing grief for the departed, as though unhappy that the person is altogether dead. This person was neither unhappy in death, nor altogether dead. Of this we were assured for good reason, including the testimony of her own words and her sincere faith.

What was it that caused such disturbing pain? I had sustained a fresh wound as I was suddenly wrenched from our most sweet and enjoyable manner of living together. I did feel joy in her testimony, when, in her last sickness, she made endearing comments about my actions and called me "dutiful." She said with great affection that she had never heard me say a harsh or reproachful word against her. But yet, O God who made us, what comparison is there between that honor I paid to her and her slavery on my behalf? Having lost such a great comfort as she was to me, my soul was wounded. Life was torn apart, since her life and mine together had been made one.

When the weeping of Adeodatus had been quieted, Euodius took up the psalter and began to sing the psalm "I will sing of mercy and judgment to You, O Lord."[9] Our whole house joined in. But hearing what we were doing, many brothers and religious women came together, while the ones whose job it was prepared the body for the burial.

In another part of the house I joined those who did not want to leave me alone and talked about something that seemed appropriate. The healing medicine of truth soothed the torment that was known only to you. They thought me to be without sorrow. But in Your ears, where none of them heard, I blamed the weakness of my feelings, and restrained my flood of grief, which gave way a little, then returned as a rising tide. It was not so overwhelming that I burst into tears or let grief show on my face. I alone knew what I was keeping down in my heart. I was very displeased to see the power that these human emotions had over me. Death must come in the due order and appointment of our natural condition.

With a new grief I grieved that I grieved, so that I was worn out by a double sorrow.

The corpse was carried to its burial. We went out and returned without tears. I still did not weep, not even in those prayers we poured forth unto You when the sacrifice of our ransom was offered for her, nor when the corpse was by the grave's side in the custom of this place, before it was laid to rest. Yet I secretly remained intensely sad the whole day. I prayed as I could, with troubled mind, that You would heal my sorrow. You did not; I think You were impressing upon my memory that the bond of all habit is strong, even in a soul that does believe deceptive ideas.

It seemed good to me to go and bathe, for I had heard that the bath took its name, the *balneum*,[10] from the Latin term for something that drives sadness from the mind. And this I confess unto Your mercy, Father of the fatherless, that I bathed, and remained the same. The bitterness of sorrow could not exude out of my heart. I slept and when I awakened my grief was softened a lot. As I lay alone with my thoughts in bed, I remembered those true verses of Ambrose.

For You are Maker of all,
the Lord and Ruler of the height,
Who, robing day in light,
have poured soft slumbers into the night,
That to our limbs the power
of toil may be renewed,
And hearts be rais'd that sink and cower,
and sorrows be subdued.

Little by little, I recovered my former thoughts of Your handmaid, her holy praise of You, her holy tenderness and observance towards us. Of this I was suddenly deprived; and I was minded to weep in Your sight for her and for myself, in her behalf and in my own. And I allowed the tears that I had restrained to overflow as much as they desired. I rested my heart upon them, and it found rest. For it was before Your eyes, not in front of men who would have scornfully interpreted my weeping. And now, Lord, in writing I confess it to You. Read it, any who will, and interpret it as you wish. If anyone finds sin in the tears I wept for my mother for a small portion of an hour, let him not berate me. This mother who now was dead to mine eyes had for many years wept for me, that I might live before Your face. If anyone feel great love for me, let him weep for all my sins against You, the Father of all the brethren of Your Christ.

But now, with a heart cured of that wound that might seem to be blameworthy earthly feeling, I poured out to You a far different kind of tears on behalf of Your handmaid. They flowed from a spirit shaken by the thoughts of the dangers of every soul that dies in Adam, although she had been quickened in Christ before her release from the flesh, and she had lived to the praise of Your name for her faith and confession. From the time You regenerated her by baptism, no word issued from her mouth against Your commandments. Your Son, the Truth, said, "Anyone who says, 'You fool!' will be in danger of the fire of hell."[11] And woe to one who lives a commendable life if they don't exercise mercy. You examine our lives. But because You are merciful in inquiring after sins, we confidently hope to find a place with You. But whosoever counts his real merits to You can count nothing but the gifts You have given to him.

O that men would know who they are as men; and that he that glories would glory in the Lord.

Laying aside her good deeds, for which I give thanks with joy, I now beseech You about the sins of mother, O, my Praise and my Life, God of my heart. Listen, I entreat You, by the medicine of the One who hung with our wounds upon the tree. He now sits at Your right hand and makes intercession to You for us. I know that she dealt mercifully, and from her heart forgave her debtors their debts. Do You also forgive her debts, whatever she may have contracted in so many years after the water of salvation? Forgive her, Lord, forgive, I beseech You; enter not into judgment with her. Let Your mercy be exalted above Your justice. Your words are true, and You have promised mercy unto the merciful, which You give us grace to be. You will have mercy on whom You will have mercy; and You will feel compassion on whom You have compassion.

And, I believe You have already done what I ask; but accept, O Lord, the offerings of my mouth, given of a free will. For when the day of her dissolution was at hand, she took no thought of having her body sumptuously wound up or embalmed with spices. She wanted no costly monument, nor did she care that she would not be buried in her own land. She asked us for none of these things. She only asked that her name might be commemorated at Your Altar, which she had served without a break of one day. She knew that holy sacrifice that would be dispensed, by which the handwriting that was against us is blotted out.

She had triumph over the enemy, who summing up our offenses and seeking what to lay to our charge, found nothing. It was all in Him in whom we conquer. Who shall restore to Him His innocent blood? Who will repay Him what He paid when He bought us and so take us from Him?

Unto the sacrament of our ransom, Your handmaid bound her soul by the bond of faith. Let none sever her from Your protection. Let neither the lion nor the dragon interpose himself by force or fraud. For she will not answer that she owes nothing, lest she be convicted and seized by the crafty accuser. Rather she will answer that her sins are forgiven her by Him, to whom none can repay what He, who owed nothing, paid for us.

May she rest then in peace with the husband before and after whom she had no man. Him she obeyed with patience, bringing forth fruit to You, that she might win him also unto You.

Inspire, O Lord, Your servants, my brethren. They are Your sons and my masters, whom with voice and heart and pen I serve. May so many as shall read these confessions at Your Altar remember Monnica, Your handmaid, with Patricius, her husband, by whose bodies You brought me into this life. May they with devout affection remember my parents in this transitory light, my brethren under You our Father in our Catholic Mother. They are my fellow citizens in that eternal Jerusalem, which Your pilgrim people sighs after from their Exodus, even unto their return. I wish that my mother's last request of me be fulfilled through my confessions more than through my prayers, that the prayers of many might be more abundantly fulfilled to her.

Notes

1. Augustine thus addressed his mother, "You, through whose prayers I firmly believe and affirm, that God gave me that mind that I should prefer nothing to the discovery of truth, wish, think of, love, naught besides. Nor do I fail to believe, that this so great good, which, through you, I have come to desire, through your prayers I shall attain" (*On the Holy Life*). He says of her, "chiefly my mother, to whom, I believe, I owe all which in me is life," and long after (*On the Gift of Perseverance*, sec. 35), "that to the faithful and daily tears of my mother, I was granted, that I should not perish."

2. Cf. Philippians 3:13.

3. Cf. 1 Corinthians 2:9 (cf. Isa. 64:4).

4. Cf. 1 Corinthians 13:9–12.

5. Cf. Revelation 21:5.

6. Matthew 25:21.

7. Cf. 1 Corinthians 15:51.

8. His name was Navigius.

9. Cf. Psalm 101.

10. *Balneum* is a generic Latin term for a public or private bath. Linguists are uncertain as to whether Augustine is correct about its derivation.

11. Cf. Matthew 5:22

The Book of Memory

I shall know You, O Lord, who know me.[1] I shall know You as I am known. Power of my soul, enter it, and fit it for You, that You may have and hold it without spot or wrinkle. This is my hope, so I speak. In this hope, I rejoice, when I rejoice in a good way. The things that are not worth tears if they be lost are all the more sorrowed for. What should be more wept for gets less concern. For behold, You love the truth, and he that does the truth comes to the light.

This truth I would set in my heart before You in confession. I would do truth in my writing before many witnesses.

Do You, my inner Physician, make clear what fruit I may reap by serving truth. I remember and confess past sins that you long ago forgave and covered, so You might bless me in You, changing my soul by faith and Your sacrament. These stir up the heart when read and heard, so the soul does not fall asleep in despair and say, "I cannot." It wakes, instead, in the love of Your mercy and the sweetness of Your grace.

By grace is the weak made strong, after he becomes conscious of his weakness.

By grace is the good delight to hear of past evils like the ones from which they have been freed. They want to hear, not because they are evil, but because they have been evil and are no longer.

With what fruit of grace then, O Lord, does one trust more in the hope of Your mercy than in personal innocence? To You my conscience must make daily confession.

With what results, I pray, do I on these pages confess to men in Your presence what I now am and not what I have been?

That old, past fruit I have seen and described.

But what I am, at the very time I make these confessions, some may want to know. Perhaps they have known me, while others may have heard from me or of me.

Whatever I have become, readers' ears are not at my heart listening in this place. Some may want to hear me confess what I am within; where neither eye nor ear nor understanding can reach. Can anyone know the heart, though they wish to and are ready to? Inner goodness will tell them that in these confessions I am not lying to them. This inner goodness believes me. But what will my words accomplish? Will people share in my joy when they hear how Your gift has brought me near to You? Will they pray for me, when they hear my weight of humanity holds back my spirit?

So I will answer these questions. It is no small product, O Lord my God, that many thanks should be given to You on our account. You have been gracious in answering our appeals. Let a brother look at me and love those things in me that you say should be loved. Let a brother mourn those things in me that You say should be lamented. Let the reader's perspective be that of brother, not of a stranger nor of strange children who only want vain talk. Their right hand is the right hand of sin. But the mind of a brother rejoices with me in what is to be approved and is sorry for what is worthy of censure. Whether in approval or reproof, the brother loves. Before such love I am willing to uncover my inner life. These who love me will delight in the goodness You have put into my life and commiserate with me that much evil remains. What is good is by Your plan and gifts. The remaining offenses are by Your judgments. Let the one bring celebration and the other sighing. Let both hymns and weeping go up to Your presence from the hearts of my brethren. Let both be sweet-smelling smoke for You.

O Lord, be pleased with the incense we burn in Your holy temple. Have mercy upon me according to Your great mercy, for Your name's sake. Do not abandon what You have begun in me, but go on to perfect all that remains unfinished.

All of this should be the result of my confessions of what I am, more than of what I have been. I will not confess this in a secret exultation that is only for Your hearing as I speak of my trembling, and my secret sorrows and hope. This is for the ears of all the believing children of humanity, that they might share in my joy as they do in my mortality. I speak for my fellow citizens and fellow pilgrims, including those who have gone to You before me and those who will come after me. All are companions of my way. These are Your servants, my brethren—those You want to be Your children. These are my masters because You commanded me to serve them if I would live in You.

Your Word would mean little to me, had He only spoken Your precepts.

But He went before me to live them.

So I am drawn along to follow.

In deed and word I follow under the shelter of Your wings.

The way would be too dangerous for me.

But You have quieted my soul under Your wings.

You know how frail I am.

No more than a child.

But my Father ever lives.

My Guardian is sufficient.

The One who gave birth to me defends me.

You Yourself are all my good. You are with me even before I am with You, so You will lead me to discover those You command me to serve.

Therefore, my confession is not what I have been, but what I now am, and the sinful person I still am. But I do not judge myself.

These are the things I would have You hear.

For You, Lord, do judge me; because, although no man knows the things of a man, but the spirit of a man that is in him,[2] yet there is something of man that not even our own spirit knows. Only You, Lord, know all of man, since You made him.

Although in Your sight I despise myself and account myself dust and ashes, I know something of You that I do not know about myself.[3] Truly we see everything through a glass darkly. We do not yet stand face to face. In this meantime when I am absent from You, I am more present with myself than with You. Yet I know that You are in all things constant; but I am unsure what temptations I can resist and where I will give in. So I hope because You are faithful and will not allow us to be tempted beyond what we can stand. You allow the temptation but make a way of escape, so we can bear it.[4]

So I will confess what I know about myself. I will confess also what I do not know. What I can discern is shown because You shine on me. What I do not know will not become clear until my darkness is like the day at noon, illuminated by Your face.

Not with doubting, but with assured consciousness, I love You, Lord. Your Word struck my heart, and I loved You. Heaven and earth and all that is in them call me from every side to love You. Creation never ceases to command all to love You, so that they have no excuse.[5] But more deeply will You have mercy on whom You will have mercy, and will have compassion on whom You have had compassion: else in deaf ears do the heaven and the earth speak Your praises.

But what do I love, when I love You?

Not beauty of bodies, nor the fair harmony of time.

Not the brightness of the light, so welcome to our eyes,

Nor sweet melodies of varied songs,

Nor the fragrant smell of flowers, and ointments and spices.

Not manna and honey, nor the embrace of arms in fleshly pleasure.

None of these I love when I love my God. Yet this love is a kind of light and melody and fragrance and meat and embrace. When I love my God, the light, melody, fragrance, meat, and embrace is experienced by my inner man. Love shines into my soul, where space cannot contain it. Love speaks with sound that does not fade into silence with time. Its smells are not dispersed in breath, and its tastes do not grow stale.

Love clings, and its satisfaction does not break my connection to the experience. This is it which I love, when I love my God.

And what is this object of my affection?

I asked the earth, and it answered, "I am not He."

All the things on earth confessed the same.

I asked the sea and the deeps, and the living creeping things.

They answered, "We are not your God. Seek above us."

I asked the wind; and the inhabitants of the sky answered, "Anaximenes was deceived. We are not God."

I asked the heavens, sun, moon, stars.

"No," they respond, "We are not the God you seek."

And I replied unto all the things that surround the door of my flesh, "You call me to my God, and you confess that you are not He. Tell me, then, something about Him."

And they cried out with a loud voice, "He made us."

My contemplation of creation posed my questions. Their beauty gave the answer.

Then I turned and looked at myself, and I asked, "Who are you?"

I answered, "A man. Look closer, and you will find a soul and a body, one inside, the other external."

By which of these ought I to seek my God? My body had looked for Him from earth to heaven, as far as I could send messengers, the gaze of my eyes.

But the better seeker is the inner being, for it was to this presiding judge that all the physical messengers reported what they had been told by heaven and earth and the things in them that had said, "We are not God, but He made us."

These things did my inner man know by the ministry of the outer. I the inner, knew them—I, the mind, learned through myself, the body.

I asked the whole frame of the world about my God. It answered, "I am not He, but He made me."

Is not this physical illustration apparent to all who have working senses? Then why does not the same message come through to all? Animals, small and great, see the world about them, but they cannot ask. No reason governs their senses to judge what their senses report. But men can ask and clearly see the invisible things of God. God can be understood by the things He made.

It is the love of the things made, instead of the Maker, that makes us subject to the world. We become subject, and those who are subject are not in a position to judge. It is only to the discerning that the creatures answer such as ask. Nor do they change their voice, their appearance. One man only sees them; another sees the same thing but asks. The same appearance speaks the same voice, yet it appears one way to this man, another way to that. To one the thing says nothing; another hears its words. Yet creation truly speaks to all. They only understand who compare the voice received from without, with the truth within.

Truth says unto me, "Neither heaven, nor earth, nor any other body is your God." Their very nature converses with Him that sees them, saying, "We are but a piece of what is. Our being is a part, not the whole."

Now to you I speak, O my soul. You are my better part, for you quicken the mass of my body, seeming to give it life. No part of creation can give life to the body. Beyond you is the God who is the Life of your life.

What then do I love, when I love my God?

Who is He who stands above the head of my soul?

By my very soul will I ascend to Him.

I will transcend the bond whereby I am united to my body.

Then all will be filled with life.

Nor can I by that power find my God, any more than a horse and mule have enough understanding to find Him. My body lives by the same power as theirs.

But there is another power. It is beyond the power that animates my flesh and gives sense to the body that the Lord designed for me. It is able to command the eye not to hear and the ear not to see. I have now a power that energizes the eye, so that through it I can see, and the ear, so that through it I should hear; and the same with the other senses. Each has their own peculiar function and purpose. Together they give a variety of information, that I the one mind can process and act upon.

I will pass beyond this power of mine that I share with the horse and mule, for they also perceive through the body.

I will pass then beyond this power of my nature, rising by degrees to Him who made me.

I come to the fields and spacious palaces of my memory. Lying all about are the treasures of innumerable images that have been collected from among impressions of all sorts, perceptions of the senses.

Besides what we think, in the memory is stored the products of sensual images collected. Some images have been enlarged and some diminished over time. What the senses bring do become changed by whatever else has been deemed important enough to lay along side. These are the things that have not been swallowed up or buried in forgetfulness.

I enter the collection, needing something there to be brought forward. Some things come forth at once. Others take a lot of searching. They must be retrieved out of some inner bin as it were. Some memories rush out in troops. One thing is desired and required, but a whole series of memories lines up, each saying, "Am I perhaps the one you are looking for?" These unwanted images must be driven away, back into the recesses, by a forceful hand of my heart. Finally what I wished for is uncovered and appears in sight from its secret place.

Other things come up readily, in unbroken order, as called for. Memories in front step aside for the ones behind. As they make way, they are hidden from sight but remain ready to come when I will. These orderly memories relate to the things I have repeated and learned by heart. Such memories have been preserved carefully, filed under categories, so that each belongs on a particular street. Some relate to light and color and form and come from the eyes. Others are sounds of all kinds, collected by the ears. Smells are brought to their avenue of memory from the nostrils, and tastes from the mouth. There is a place for touch sensations from the whole body, relating to what is hard and soft; hot or cold; smooth or rugged; or heavy or light. Senses record whether these are things outward or inward to the body.

This is a picture of that great harbor of the memory, which has numberless secret and inexpressible windings, where things are kept to be brought out at need. Each enters in by its proper gate and is laid up. But it isn't the things themselves that enter in, just their perceived images, for thought to recall. Who really understands these images and how they are formed? It is plain what senses stored up each memory.

Even while I dwell in darkness and silence, in my memory I can produce colors if I want, and discern between black and white and other hues if I wish. This happens without sound breaking in to distract me from reviewing the image before my eyes, even though sounds also are there, lying dormant, apart from the sight images. If I also call for these, soon they appear. And though my tongue be still, and my throat mute, I can sing as I wish.

Nor do these images of colors that are there intrude and interrupt when another store is called for of sounds that flowed in by the ears. So the other things, piled in and up by the other senses, I recall at my pleasure. By this means, I can discern the smell of lilies from violets while I am smelling neither. I prefer the taste of honey to the taste of sweet wine. I know what is smooth and want it rather than what is rugged. All the while, nothing am I tasting or touching. I'm remembering.

Thoughts occur inside me, in that vast court of my memory. Inside my mind exist heaven, earth, sea, and whatever I can think about them. Even what I have forgotten is hidden there. I must go there to meet with myself, to recall what I am like, and what I have done, where and when and what feelings resulted. Here is found all I remember, either of my own experience or of what others have done.

Out of the same store do I combine past thoughts with new, fresh ideas and likenesses. I add new experiences to old; new beliefs to those things I once believed. There I can infer future actions and events from my hopes. In the present I reflect on, I decide to myself, "I will do this or that." It all takes place in that great receptacle of my mind, which gives storage for so many and such great images. I reason that "this or that will follow" upon another occurrence. I state the desire, "O that this or that might be!" Or I pray, "God, keep this or that from happening!" So speak I to myself. When I speak, the images of all I speak about are at hand, taken out of the same treasury of memory. I could not say such things if the images of memory were not there.

Great is the force of memory. It is a very great influence, O my God, such a large and boundless chamber.

Who ever probed the bottom of it? Yet is this my power? It is part of my nature, nor can I myself comprehend all that I am.

I must conclude that the mind is too limited to contain even itself. And what is the part that the mind cannot contain in itself? Is it outside the mind itself, rather than hidden within? If it is there, why can't I comprehend it?

I tell you a great marvel. Amazement seizes me to think that men go abroad to admire the heights of mountains, the mighty billows of the sea, the broad tides of rivers, the compass of the ocean and the circuits of the stars. Yet they ignore the wonder found in themselves. They do not think it wondrous that I can speak of all these things, yet they are not in front of my eyes. I can speak of experiencing them, because I actually have seen the mountains, billows, rivers, and stars. And there is an ocean that I believe exists. All these things come from inside me in my memory. I can visualize the same vast spaces as if I saw them abroad. When I did see such things, I drew them into myself. I do not need them with me in themselves, because I have their images in my mind. And I know by what body senses each of these made an impression upon me.

But my memory retains more than these things in its immeasurable capacity. My mind also remembers all of the liberal science knowledge that I have not forgotten. These facts have been removed to an inner place, which truly is no physical location. These cannot even be reduced to physical images, but I keep these bits of knowledge as the things themselves.

For, what is literature or the art of disputing? How many kinds of questions are there? Everything I know on such subjects exists in my memory. It is not that I have reduced the facts to an image, and left out the thing itself. It is not as if the facts made a sound and then passed away, like the sound of a voice that has been fixed on the ear. This is not the same as remembering a sound after it has ceased resonating or a smell after it evaporates into air and no longer affects the sense of smell. Such things convey into memory images. Remembering the image, we can renew our experience with it. It is like meat that has no taste when it reaches the stomach, yet the memory holds its taste and plays over its enjoyment. It is as anything the body perceives by touch. When the object is removed, memory of the touch still moves us. None of the like experiences are themselves transmitted into memory. Only their images remain. With an admirable swiftness they are caught up, and stored as in wondrous cabinets. The act of remembering brings forth these things wonderfully.

But not all memories are images. I hear that there are three kinds of questions: (1) Does something actually exist? (2) What is it? (3) What kind is it? I do indeed hold the images of the sounds of which those words are composed. I remember that these sounds with a noise passed through the air and then ceased.

But what of the ideas communicated by those sounds? I have not experienced them through the senses of my body. I have never "seen" them, except in my mind. No images of these things are in my memory. Rather, since they are ideas, the things themselves are in me. How did they enter into me? Let them say if they can. For I have gone over all the avenues of my flesh, but cannot find the one by which they entered. For the eyes say, "If those images were colored, we reported it." The ears say, "If they sound, we passed on that knowledge." The nostrils say, "If they smell, they passed through us." The tongue says, "Unless these ideas have a flavor, don't ask me." The touch says, "If it has no mass, I didn't handle it, and if I didn't handle it, I passed along no information of it."

How and from where did these things enter my memory? I do not know. For when I learned them, I gave not credit to another man's mind, but recognized them in mine. I decided that they were true and commended them to myself, laying them up from where I might bring them to mind when I wished. In my heart then they were, even before I learned them, but in my memory they were not. Why, when they were spoken, did I acknowledge them and say, "So it is. This is true," unless they were already in the memory? If so, the facts were so discarded, as in deeper recesses, that had not someone else suggested them and drawn them out, I likely would never have conceived the thought.

So, we find that some things that have no sensible images must be learned by perceiving the thing itself within us. We must take in the thing as it is in itself, without images, receiving nothing but the conception.

We do this by gathering all those related thoughts that the memory had randomly collected and stored. These were laid up without a plan or arrangement, but now the mind assembles these fragments, almost as if in a single memory from where they had lain unknown, scattered and neglected. Now the mind looks at them and familiarizes itself with them.

Think how many such thoughts are carried about in the memory. These are all the things that have been learned and now are organized so that they can come to hand. These are things we are said to have learned and come to know, though after a short time we may have stopped thinking about them. They are buried. They have been pushed back, deeper and deeper, into the recesses. But they can be brought out again as if new, to be thought out in different ways.

These ideas have no other home than the mind. They must be drawn together again that they may be known. That is to say, they must, as it were, be collected from their dispersion.

Thus the word *cogitation* is derived. For *cogo* ("I collect") and *cogito* ("I think or re-collect") have the same relation to each other as *ago* ("I do") and *agito* ("I keep doing"), or *facio* ("I make") and *factito* ("I continually make"). But the mind has appropriated to itself this word *cogitation*, so that what is "collected" and then "recollected," brought together, in the mind, is properly said to be "cogitated," or thought upon.

The memory contains also the countless principles and laws that govern work with numbers and dimensions. None of these has in any bodily sense been impressed upon the mind. Numbers have neither color nor sound nor taste nor smell nor touch. I have heard the sound of the words whereby these rules can be explained, but the sounds are different than the things signified. The sounds are much different in Greek, for example, than in Latin. But the things are neither Greek, nor Latin, nor any other language. I have seen lines made by the finest architects, strokes as precise and narrow as a spider's thread. But those drawings are still not the images nor physical laws depicted by those lines. This my physical eyes showed me. The eye knows the difference. Anyone who understands geometric laws learns to recognize them within the self.

I have perceived also the numbers by which we count and work mathematics. The things enumerated may register on the senses of my body, but not the numbers by which the things are counted. Number is different from what is numbered. One contains no image of the other, but both what is numbered and the numbers have their own forms of existence. They are. Let him who laughs at me that he does not see the numbers go ahead and laugh at me for saying things like this.

While he makes fun of me, I will pity him.

All these things I remember, and how I learned them I remember. I also remember the false objections made against these precepts. Although other theories are false, it is not false that I remember them. I remember also that I have discerned between the truths and the false objections. And I perceive that the present discerning of these things differs from the memories of past times when I often thought the various arguments through and decided which were true. I both remember past understandings and my discernments and understandings of today. I lay today's thoughts in my memory, so later I may remember what I understand now. I remember that I have remembered, so that later I shall be able to call these memories to remembrance. I shall remember that I have now been able to remember through the force of my memory.

The same memory can recall the emotions that were in my mind at each time of life. My memory holds these affections in a different sense than my mind experiences them. The memory has a power over emotions that my mind lacks, so that the remembering is far different than the experiencing. Without rejoicing, I remember the joys I once felt. Without renewed sorrow, I recollect past sorrows. I can review old fears without being afraid and remember what I once wanted without new desire. In reflecting on some memories, I now feel the opposite emotion I felt then. I remember with joy an old sorrow and feel sorrow about the fact that I once counted certain things to be joys. This is not so surprising as it relates to physical passions, for mind is one thing and body another. If I can feel happy now about some past bodily pain, it isn't something to be wondered at. This memory relating to body now relates to reason. When we decide to give our memory a special charge to keep something, we say, "Be sure to keep that in mind." When we try to recall some forgotten thing, we say, "That did not come to my mind" and "It slipped out of my mind." So we naturally identify the memory with the mind.

How is it, then, that when with joy I remember my past sorrow, the mind experiences a joy while the memory retains the sorrow, yet loses the sadness? The mind is affected by the joyfulness in it and is joyful. The memory fixes upon the sadness in it but is not sad.

Does the memory perhaps not belong to the mind? Who will try to argue that?

No, the memory is, as it were, the *belly* of the mind. Joy and sadness are like sweet and bitter food. Once committed to memory, it is as if these emotions are passed into the belly. There they can be stowed but not tasted. As ridiculous as it seems to equate memories of joy and sorrow, they are not utterly dissimilar.

Here is an example. Out of my memory I bring to mind the past thought that there are four states of feeling that can agitate the mind—desire, joy, fear, and sorrow. I can bring from memory disputations that this is not so. I can try to divide each of the four into subordinate groups and redefine them, but I remember former reasoning that defeat the alternative ideas.

So I can bring these states of mind to awareness and contemplate their effects, yet I can reason about these influences on the mind without being influenced in mind by them. I can call them to mind, remember what I know of them, and recall when I felt them. I can remember past times when I called them from memory and thought about them. They were there by recollection, perhaps in the way some animals can bring food out of the belly to chew on it again as cud.

These states of mind are recalled out of memory. But they are different, or else how could a debater recall and almost taste these states yet keep the mind untouched by them? Does the mind by musing feel the sweetness of joy or the bitterness of sorrow? Does the analogy of the animal's cud not work because there are some differences between the two realities? Who would willingly speak of some hard thought, be it a grief or fear, if by considering it one had to become sad or fearful? In fact, we could not properly speak of them if we did not find such experiences in our memory.

The memory stores not only the sounds of the names of these states according to the images impressed by the senses of the body. Actual notions of the very things themselves which we never received by any avenue of the body are there. These are processed thoughts that were stored when the mind itself did experience these states by its own passions. Observations about the experience were committed to memory, or the memory of the moment itself is retained. Yet the memory does not have to commit to the feelings.

Are these images or not? Who can readily say? I name a stone. I name the sun. The things themselves are not present to my senses, but their images are available to my memory. I name a bodily pain that I do not now feel. Nothing aches. Yet unless the image of the pain were present to my memory, I should not know what to say about it. I could not even discuss how to tell this pain from pleasure. I speak of bodily health while healthy in body. Now the thing I am talking about is present with me.

Yet, unless some image of what I have experienced in bodily health were in memory, I could not by experience alone recall precisely what the concept means. The sick could not speak of the meaning of health, unless some image of what "health" means attached itself by force of memory when the thing itself were absent from the body. I can name numbers whereby we count, but not their images. Only the words themselves have meanings present in my memory. I name the image of the sun, and an image is present in my memory. I recall not the image of its image, but the image itself is present to me, calling it to mind. I name "memory," and I recognize what I name. How do I recognize it except in the memory of memory in itself?

Is it also present to itself in its image, and not in itself?

❧

Great is the power of memory. Its force is a fearful thing, a deep and boundless exhibition. Here is the mind, and a view of what I myself am.

What am I then, O my God? What nature am I? The aspects of life are varied, numerous, and very immense. Just explore the plains, tunnels, and caverns of memory. Memories are innumerable and innumerably full of innumerable kinds of things. Memories are filled with images and being. The things themselves are present as in a remembered performance of the arts, or being is reduced to some ideas and impressions, in the case of emotions the mind has felt. Even when the mind no longer feels, the memory retains. Yet whatsoever is in the memory is also in the mind. The mind can call to thought and run through all of the related memories. It can fly through them or dive this way and that to pull them together. There is no end of what can be done. So great is the force of memory, so great the force of life, even in the mortal life of man.

What shall I do then, O my true life? I will pass beyond this power of mine which is called memory. I will pass beyond it so that I can approach You, O sweet Light. What do You have to tell me? I am climbing through my mind to reach out toward You who exist above me. I now will pass beyond this power of mine called memory because I want to arrive at You. Wherever it is that You may be found and clung to, there I will cling to You. You even made the animals and birds to have memory, or else they could not return to their dens and nests, nor know how to go about their many other activities. Nor indeed could they become accustomed to anything, except by memory.

I will pass then beyond memory also, that I may arrive at Him who made me separate from the four-footed beasts and made me wiser than the fowl of the air. I will pass beyond memory also to where I shall find You, You truly good and certain sweetness. Where shall I find You? I find You without my memory, but I retain You in my memory. How shall I find You, if I cannot remember You?

For the woman that had lost her valued coin and sought it with a light; unless she had remembered it, she would never have found it.[6] For when it was found, how did she know whether it was the same coin, except by her memory? I have remembered to seek and find many a lost thing; so I know that when I was seeking something I would see things and ask myself, "Is this it?" "Is that what I am looking for?" My mind would keep telling me that each find was not, until that one thing was seen that I sought. Had I not remembered the specific thing in question, I would not have found it, even if it were offered to me. I could not recognize it.

So it ever is when we seek and find any lost thing. Something that is by chance lost from the sight is not lost from the memory. Its image is there, like that of any visible body. The image is retained within and sought until it is restored to sight. When it is found, it is recognized by comparison to the image that is kept within. Nor do we say that we have found what was lost unless we recognize it. We cannot recognize it unless we remember it. We cannot remember it unless what was lost to the eyes was retained in the memory.

But what about when the memory itself loses the image? So it happens that we have to seek out the thing itself so that our mind can make an image of it once more. Where in the end do we search, but in the memory itself? And if one thing is offered instead of what we want, we still have enough image in memory that we can reject all other things until we are reacquainted with the one thing we are looking for. Then we say, "This is it." We should not be able to do that unless we recognized it. We could not recognize it unless we retained some memory of it.

Certainly we had forgotten it, but the whole had not escaped us. Was the lost part sought for on the basis of the part we still retained? The memory felt it did not possess all of the image that was required. It felt handicapped, unable to fulfill its ancient work of remembering until the missing part was restored. For instance, if we see or think of someone we know, but we cannot recall his name, we try to recover it no matter what. We search through the mind for names, but nothing connects itself to the person. The mind then has enough of a memory to know what is not the correct name, because the name does not belong with the familiar person and so is rejected. Then a name presents itself that comfortably fits the person in knowledge. That name and its connection came from the memory itself. Even if we do not recognize the name until someone else reminds us, the fact that we know it is the right name for the person comes from memory. We hear the name and do not accept that it is a new fact. It is a once recognized fact and we know it is the correct name. Were it utterly blotted out of the mind, we should not remember it, even when reminded. For we have not as yet utterly forgotten what we remember that we have forgotten. When we have utterly forgotten, we cannot seek what is lost.

How then do I seek You, O Lord?

For when I seek You, my God, I seek a happy life.

I seek You that my soul may live.

For my body lives by my soul.

And my soul lives by You.

How then do I seek a happy life, seeing I have it not, until I can say, where I ought to say it, "It is enough"?

How do I seek it?

By remembering as though I had forgotten it?

By remembering that I had forgotten it?

By desiring to learn about it as a thing that until now was unknown?

Is it unknown because I have never really known?

Or is it unknown because I have utterly forgotten it?

Am I unable to remember even that I had forgotten it?

Don't all people want a happy life?

Does anyone really not want it?

How can they know to seek it unless they have some image in memory of what the concept of a happy life looks like? How do they know it enough to desire it? Have they seen it before to know that it would be a desirable thing to have? Truly we have that memory; how, I do not know.

Apart from other states of mind, there is a way of living that is happiness. Others are blessed with a hope for happiness. These who hope have a lower kind of happiness than they who truly experience it. Yet those who hope are better off than those who have neither the experience or the hope. Even those who lack hope, though, have an image that there is such a thing as happiness, or else they would not desire it. It is certain that all people do want to be happy.

Unless we knew it, we could not want it. I don't know how, but all have some sort of knowledge of goodness. I am mystified as to whether it is built into the memory. Could it be that we have a shared human memory from he who was truly happy before he first sinned? In the sin of that first man we all died. From that man we inherited our birth into misery; I only ask whether it is possible that the same person passed to us the memory of what it means to have a happy life. I ask that because of the argument that we should not love the idea of being happy if we had no awareness of it. We hear the name, and we all confess that we desire the thing.

The mere sound of the word *happiness* is not automatically delightful. When a Greek hears it in Latin, he is not delighted. Without understanding Latin, he doesn't even know that he heard the word. But we who know Latin hear the same word and do feel delight, the same delight that the Greek speaker would feel if he heard the word spoken in Greek. From this we know that the concept itself is not restricted to expression in Greek or Latin.

The word is not the thing in itself, or else people of all other tongues would not long for it so earnestly. The concept is universally known. Could all people with one voice be asked, "Do you desire happiness?" all would answer, without doubt, "We do." And this could not be, unless the thing itself whereof it is the name were retained in the memory.

Is this the same kind of memory one has of Carthage after having once seen the city?

No. A happy life is not seen with the eye, because it is not the thing that we remember.

So do we remember it the way we remember the experience of numbers?

No. The person lacks direct contact with the thing itself of which there is knowledge. The person who remembers the concepts of what numbers are does not seek to attain them experientially, not the way that the person wants the happy life that exists conceptually in our knowledge. We know to love happiness and still desire to attain it, that we may be happy.

Is it the same way we remember eloquence then?

No. For although people hear this name and have some understanding of the concept, yet that still does not make anyone eloquent. Many who desire to be eloquent seem to have a certain level of knowledge in their memory. On closer examination, though, one finds that they have had direct contact with eloquence through their bodily senses. They have seen and heard others be eloquent, and it was a delight. They desired to do the things that had given them joy through sensory experience. Had they not had the sensory experience, they would not have had the delight. Without inward knowledge of rhetoric they would not have wished to be like what they heard.

This is not like our desire for a happy life, for we do not have sensory experience of it in others.

Do we have the memory of the happy life as we have the memory of joy?

Perhaps it is something like that. I remember what joy is like, even when I am sad. I have a concept of living a happy life when I am unhappy. I did not with bodily senses see, hear, smell, taste, or touch joy. I experienced it in my mind in moments of rejoicing, and the knowledge of it clung to the memory. I may recall some moments when I felt joy and now I feel disgust that I once rejoiced. Other memories bring a longing. It depends on what I now consider joyful as opposed to what I once found to be joy. Once there were foul things that immersed me in a sort of joy. Recalling those now, I detest and curse those things. It is the memory of good and honest joys that now I recall with longing. These I may not be able to relive, so it is with a kind of sadness that I recall the former joy.

But where and when did I experience my happy life, that I should remember it and love and long for it? Nor is this just my own experience or that of only a few. We all would like to be happy. Unless we had some certain knowledge to know the meaning of happiness, we should not want it with so firm a resolve.

Two men are asked whether they would like to be a soldier in a war. One might answer that he would like to do that, while the other would not want to do it. Yet if both were asked whether they would like to be happy, either would instantly and without any doubt say that he would. In fact, for no other reason would the one go to war, and the other not, except to pursue what they think might bring happiness to them. Perhaps as one looks for his joy in this thing and another in that, all agree their desire to seek joy is so that they might be happy. Wouldn't anyone, if asked, express the wish to have joy and call that joy a happy life? One looks for this joy by one means and another by another means, but all have the same end toward which they strive, the end of joy.

Joy being a thing that all seek and so must say they have experienced, it is therefore found in the memory, and recognized whenever the concept of a happy life is mentioned.

But Lord, keep me far from one error. May it be far from the heart of Your servant who here confesses unto You, that I should feel momentary earthly joy and suppose that I had reached true happiness. There is a joy that brings true happiness, but it is not given to the ungodly. It is only for those who love You for Your own sake.

That joy is to know You as You are. This is the happy life, to rejoice in You, of You, and for You. This is the happy life, and there is no other. They who think there is another, pursue some other. They are not on the track of true joy. Yet they still have that image of it inside that makes them run after what looks like some semblance of the real joy.

It is by no means certain that all wish the happiness that is true joy, for that means finding joy in You, the only hope of a happy life. No, not all want the happy life this way. Or perhaps it is more accurate to say that all want happiness, but because the flesh lusts against the Spirit, and the Spirit against the flesh, they cannot do what they fundamentally want. So they latch onto something that looks like happiness where they can and try to be content with it. They are not able to want true joy. Their human will does not have a strong enough desire to make them able to want real happiness.

Now I can ask anyone whether he would rather experience joy in truth, or in a lie. He will no more hesitate to say, "In the truth," as he hesitated to say, "I want to be happy." But the happy life is joy in the truth, and joy in the truth is only joy in You, who are the Truth. O God my Light, You alone bring health to my life. This is the happy life that all desire. This is the only life that is happy, so it is the life that all really want. And all want to find true joy. I have met many who wanted to deceive others. I have met not one who outwardly wished to be deceived.

So we add this to our investigation, that people have an image of the concept of a happy life and they also have, evidently from the same place, gained a knowledge of the concept of truth as well. They also must love truth, because they do not want to be deceived. And they love the concept of a happy life, which is found nowhere other than through joying in the truth. They love the truth, which they would not love, were there not some notice of it in their memory.

Why then does no one without help find the joy that comes in truth? Why are they not happy? It is because they are more strongly taken up with things that have more power to make them miserable, and they only faintly remember the Source of happiness. There is yet a little light in men, so let them walk. Let them walk, that the darkness does not overtake them.

In fact, rather than movement toward happiness, why does truth generate hatred? When a servant of Yours teaches the truth he makes enemies of those who profess to want a happy life. Yet the happy life that is desired comes only with finding joy in the truth. This paradox is possible because people have become twisted in their love for truth, so that they will only love the truth that they have decided to be true. They would gladly accept as truth what they have decided that they love. Since they don't want to be deceived, they refuse to be convinced that anything other than what they believe is so.

Therefore, in the end they hate the truth for the sake of what they love in the place of the truth. They love truth that enlightens, they hate truth that reproves. Since they would not be deceived, yet would deceive others, they love truth when she uncovers herself to benefit them. They hate her when she uncovers them. Truth shall give them their justice in the end. Those who do not want truth about themselves to be revealed will be revealed for who they are against their will. Yet they will not by this uncovering discern anything about the nature of truth.

Look and know; yes, see the human mind at work.

Look at it, blind and sick, foul and ugly.

How it wishes its intentions to remain hidden.

How it wants to see all else revealed but itself.

Now hear the judgment rendered:

The mind will not be hidden from truth.

But truth is hid from it.

Yet even in this miserable state there is hope, for still there is in the heart a desire for joy in truths and not in lies. Happy is the one, when distractions are removed, who is allowed to come to joy in that only Truth, by whom all things are true.

I have now gone a long way in contemplating the memory and the search for You, O Lord. Beyond these bounds I have not found You. Nor have I found anything concerning You, but what I have kept in memory, ever since I learned about You. For since I learned about You, I have not forgotten You. Where I found truth, there I found my God, the Truth itself. This much I have learned and not forgotten. Since I learned about

You, You live in my memory. There I find You when I call You to remembrance, and delight in You.

These are my holy delights, which You have given me in Your mercy because You took pity on my poverty.

But where in my memory do you live, O Lord?

Where do You make Your home there?

What manner of lodging have You framed?

What sanctuary have You built?

You have given this honor to my memory, that You have taken up residence there, but I cannot point out the neighborhood in which You live, however deeply I consider the matter. For in thinking on You, I have moved beyond those mental capacities that I share with the animals. I have not found You among the images of material life I have collected. Nor have I found you in those places where I store the memories of remembered desires in my mind. I have entered the very seat of my mental function, where the memory is able to remember itself and its reasoning. You were not there.

For You are not a mental image, or the affection of a living being, as when I rejoice, console, desire, fear, remember, forget, and such things. Neither are You the mind itself. You are the Lord God of the mind. All my thoughts and emotions change, but You transcend all of that and do not change. Yet You have given Yourself to dwell in my memory, since I learned You. So why am I even seeking to find the place of Your dwelling, as if there are cubicles to contain You inside of me? I do have certainty that You are there, since I have remembered

You ever since I learned You. All I need in order to find You is to call You to remembrance.

Where then did I find You, that I might learn You? You were not in my memory before I learned You. You were far above me, so how could I find You by learning You? I look backward and forward in my mind, and I see no place. Rather, the answer is that *everywhere* You give audience to all who ask counsel of You. You initiate conversation with all, whatever the varied ways they ask to gain Your counsel. You make Your answers clear. The problem is that not all clearly hear. All in some way consult You, according to what they are willing to ask. Not all are able to hear beyond what they desire to hear.

Your true servant listens to hear from You what he wants, and wants to hear what You say.

Too late I loved You.[7]

O you Beauty of ancient days, yet ever new!

Too late I loved You.

Look, You were within, and I was out wandering, searching.

I was a monster, plunging through Your fair artistry.

You were with me, but I was not with You.

A world of things hindered me from finding You.

Yet such things have no existence unless they are in You.

You called, shouted, and burst my deafness.

You flashed, shone, and scattered my blindness.

You breathed out wondrous odors.

Finally I drew in my breath and craved Your aroma.
I tasted until I knew hunger and thirst.

You touched me, and I burned for Your peace.

One day with all of my self I shall be able to cling to Your being. Then I shall put aside sorrow and labor; and my life will wholly live, for I will be wholly full of You. But even now You fill the one You lift up. I am aware that I am not full of You, so I am a burden to myself. Lamentable joys contend with joyous sorrows. Which will win the contest? How can I know?

Woe is me!

Lord, have pity upon me.

My evil sorrows battle my good joys,

until it is hard to know what will win.

Woe is me! Lord, have pity upon me.

Woe is me, for I am sick.

I will not hide my wounds from You the Physician.

You are merciful, but I am miserable.

Is not the life of man upon earth all trial? Who wishes for troubles and difficulties? You command them to be endured, not to be loved. No man loves what he endures, though he may indeed love to endure. For though he rejoices that he endures, he had rather there were nothing for him to endure. In adversity I long for prosperity, in prosperity I fear adversity. What middle place is there betwixt these two, where the life is not all trial?

Woe to the prosperity of the world, once and again, through fear of adversity, and corruption of joy! Woe to the adversities of the world, which are experienced again and again and again in the longing for prosperity and the hardness of adversity. Such life forces are able to shatter our ability to endure. Is not the life of man upon earth trial without respite?

Such a reality allows hope in nothing except Your exceedingly great mercy. Give us what You command us to have, and You can command anything You want to. You command chastity, and I am one who says that none can remain chaste except God give the gift of chastity. This lesson was part of the wisdom I needed in order to live, and I learned the Source of the gift. By chastity we are truly bound and led back into unity, where in dissipation we led a fragmented life. Too little does he love You, who loves You along with everything else.[8]

O Love, who ever burns and never consumes.

Kindle me with new affections, O my God.

You call me to purity, so give me what You command, and command what You will.

That is a mournful darkness, whereby the abilities within me are hidden from me. My mind seeks inside itself for strength and does not venture to believe that there is any power to resist evil. The power there is mostly hidden, unless experience reveals it. And no one ought to feel sure in that life, all of which is called a trial, of being able to move in personal discipline from worse to better. It is as likely he will move from better to worse.

The delights of the ear at one time firmly entangled me, but You did loosen and free me. Now, in those melodies that Your words breathe soul into, when sung with a sweet and attuned voice, I do a little repose. Yet I am not so held by them that I cannot disengage myself when I want to. The words that are their life find their way into my heart, so that I can esteem them with suitable value due to them.

At one time I believe I gave them more honor than is seemly. I believed that our minds became more holy and were raised to a more fervent flame of devotion by the holy words themselves when sung than when not. I felt that the varied feelings of the spirit were given sweet variety when they were properly voiced in singing, as if some hidden special work in them was stirred up.

But this contentment in the flesh can be debilitating to the soul, which must not be given over to it. There is a beguiling sense in which I would rather not give myself to thought, so as to submissively follow her leading. The emotional response has been allowed in to serve reason, but it always wants to run before thought and lead the way. So sin can come in unaware, and I am only afterwards aware of it.

At other times, I am so wary of being drawn into error that I avoid this deception by becoming too strict. Rejecting music also is an error, and sometimes I have wished to banish from my ears all the melodies of sweet music in David's psalter. I would deny it to the Church's ears too, for that seems safer. I remember hearing often of the concern in this regard of Athanasius, Bishop of Alexandria.[9] He made the reader of the psalm utter it with so little inflection of voice that it was nearer speaking than singing.

Then I remember the tears I shed at the psalmody of Your church when I first recovered faith. I am moved, not so much with the singing as with the words sung. When they are sung with a clear voice and suitable modulation, I acknowledge the value of this institution.

Thus, in regard to the singing, my opinion fluctuates between allowing the peril of pleasure or staying with the more approved wholesomeness. I incline to the latter, though not with an irrevocable judgment that singing should not be approved in the church. Its delight of the ears does help weaker minds rise to devotion. Yet when it happens that I am more moved by the voice than the words sung, I confess that I have sinned penally. It would be better then if I did not hear music. See this problem and empathize. Weep for me especially, you who are better able to regulate your feelings, so that only a good outcome ensues. I know that some are not drawn into the music, so that these things do not touch you.

But You, O Lord, my God, listen. Behold and see and have mercy and heal me, You in whose presence I sometimes become a problem to myself. This is my infirmity.

There remains the pleasure of the eyes that I need to confess in the hearing of the ears of Your temple, those brotherly and devout ears. With the eyes I conclude considerations of the temptations of the lust of the flesh that still assail me. I groan earnestly, desiring to be enclosed with my house from heaven.

The eyes love fair and varied forms, and bright and soft colors. Let not these things occupy my soul. Rather, let God occupy it who made these things very good indeed. He is my good, not they. And these sights affect me, from waking through the whole day. Nor is there any escape from beauty as I can find from musical temptations by seeking silence from all voices. The queen of colors, the light, bathes all we behold everywhere through the day. Light glides by me in varied forms, soothing me when I am engaged in harder things, even when I cannot take time to notice it. So strongly does light and color entwine through life that if light is suddenly withdrawn I long for it, and my mind becomes depressed if it is missing for any length of time.

To this might be added another form of temptation that is more directly dangerous. There is that lust of the flesh that consists in the delight of all senses and pleasures, wherein its slaves go far from You, waste and perish. But the soul also has, through the same senses of the body, a certain vain and curious desire to study and experiment in fleshly things. This temptation becomes veiled under the category of knowing and learning. It is not so much a matter of delighting in the flesh. Here is an appetite for knowledge, and sight is the foremost sense used for attaining knowledge. It is in divine language the lust of the eyes.

To "see" is properly the work of the eyes, but we use this word to relate to the other senses when we employ them in seeking knowledge. We do not say, "Hear how it flashes." "Smell how it glows." "Taste how it shines." "Feel how it gleams." All these are said to be seen. Yet we do not only say, "See how it shines," as if the eyes alone can perceive. We might also say, "See how it sounds." "See how it smells." "See how it tastes." "See how hard it is." So the general experience of the senses becomes the lust of the eyes. The eyes hold the first place in the office of seeing, but the other senses take on similar works of perception as they search after knowledge of their surroundings.

More may become evident about this lust when we discern that curiosity is one of the pleasures that is an object of the senses. Pleasure seeks to find objects that are beautiful, fragrant, savory, and soft. Curiosity, for the sake of trying things out, will try out objects that are not pleasant. The senses are called upon, not for the sake of putting them through annoying experiences, but out of a lust to know the nature of the objects around us.

What pleasure does it give to see a mangled carcass that will make you shudder? Yet when one is lying near, people flock to it. It makes them sad or turns them pale. The memory of it disturbs their sleep with fears. It is as if they had been compelled to experience death when they were awake, or as if someone reported to them how beautiful it was, so they had to see it for themselves. The same is true of the other senses should we take the time to reason through examples.

It is to stimulate this disease of curiosity that all sorts of strange sights are exhibited in the theater. Hence men go on to search out the hidden powers of nature (a side issue we won't consider). It doesn't profit anyone to experience these shows; it only feeds on the desire to know the experience. It is in search of the same perverted knowledge that people inquire into occult arts. People want the same kinds of experiences from religion, as when they try to tempt God to produce the signs and wonders they demand. The magical experience is not desired for any good end, but merely to try it.

In this vast wilderness, there are a multitude of snares and dangers. Many of them I have cut off and thrust out of my heart. You have given me the strength to do it as God of my salvation. Still I dare to admit that all sorts of enticements buzz on all sides around our daily life. Can I yet say that nothing of this sort engages my attention or causes in me an idle interest? True, the theater no longer carries me away. I do not care to know the courses of the stars. I have never been tempted to consult departed ghosts. Such sacrilegious mysteries I detest. By what tricks and suggestions does the enemy lure me to desire some sign from You, O Lord my God, to whom I owe humble and single-hearted service? I still petition on behalf of submission to my King of the pure and holy Jerusalem that I be kept from consenting to any such thing. May these ideas be moved farther and farther from me. When I ask You for the salvation of anyone, it is not my aim and intention to have a sign; it is far different than that. You give and will give me grace to follow You willingly. You will help me do what You desire of me.

Setting aside victories, in how many petty, contemptible matters is our curiosity daily tempted? Who can remember how often we give in? How often do we start to allow people to tell worthless stories in our midst, lest we offend them? Then we discover that we have taken a curious interest in the silliness. I no longer go to the circus to see a dog chasing a rabbit. But if I am passing a field where a chase is underway, I may well be distracted from some weighty thought. It is not that I turn aside my animal to watch, but I incline my mind in that direction. I might dully stop and watch if You did not make me see this weakness and quickly warn me, either by the sight itself or by drawing my attention towards You.

What if, while I sit at home my attention is attracted by a lizard catching flies or a spider entangling them in her nets? Is the thing different because they are but small creatures? I go on from them to praise You, the wonderful Creator and Orderer of all, but this does not first draw my attention. It is one thing to rise quickly, another not to fall.

My life is full of pettiness; my one hope is Your wondrously great mercy.[10] When our heart becomes the receptacle of such things and is overcharged with a swarm of this uselessness that is all about, then prayers are often interrupted and distracted. When we enter Your presence we are in the very matter of directing the voice of our heart to Your ears. Look how great a matter is broken off by the rushing in of idle thoughts. Shall we really consider this to be a problem of slight concern, or will anything bring us back to a true perception except Your full mercy, the mercy that continues to change us?

And You know how far You have already come in changing me. You first healed me of the lust of feeling that I must defend my honor. After you broke this self-justification, You could make me confront the rest of my sins. Only then could I find healing from my infirmities, redemption from corruption, and a crown of mercy and pity. Only then could You satisfy my desire with good things. You first had to curb my pride with fear of You, and train my neck to fit into Your yoke. Now that I have learned to bear the yoke, it feels light. So You promised, and have made it. The promise was there at the start, but I did not comprehend when I was afraid to submit to Your will.

You alone, Lord, are without pride, because You are the only true Lord, who needs to submit to no lord. Has this temptation also ceased in me, or can it cease through my life? There is a wish, namely to be feared and loved of men, that has no other purpose but to bring personal joy. Such a joy is no joy but a miserable life of foul boasting. But it comes as a trap to keep people from loving or fearing You with purity. And therefore do You resist the proud, and give grace to the humble. You thunder down upon the ambitions of the world, and the foundations of the mountains tremble.[11]

Because now certain endeavors of human society encourage praise and love and respect, the adversary of our true blessedness is at hand. Everywhere he is spreading his snares of "Well done! Good job!" He catches us at a point where we are greedy. In the search for importance, we may be taken unawares, and our joy of ego separates us from Your truth. We are caught in the deceptions of manipulators because we love to be loved and feared. It does not please us to gather praise for Your sake, but we take it in Your place. By such traps men become like another master, that he may have them for his own, not in the chains of love, but in shackles of punishment. He first proposed to set his throne in the north, that he might be served where it is dark and chilled, in a perverse and bent imitation of You.

But we, O Lord, are Your little flock. Possess us as Yours.

Stretch Your wings over us and let us fly under them.

Be our glory.

May we be Your love?

May Your words be our reverence?

Any who would be praised of men, will men defend them from Your charge? Will men deliver when You judge and condemn? We know the sinner is not praised for the desires of his soul, nor blessed who does what is not godly. More subtle is the fault when someone is praised for some gift that You have given him. He may begin to rejoice more at the praise he receives for using the gift well than You are honored for giving the gift that caused him to be praised. He is praised, while You do not receive due honor.

So better is the one who praised than one who is praised. The one took pleasure in the gift of God in a man. The other was better pleased with the gift of man, than of God. By these temptations we are assailed daily, O Lord. We are continually attacked. Our daily furnace of affliction is the praising tongue of others.

In this way, You command us to purity as well. Give what You command, and command what You want. You know how my heart groans about this. My eyes flood. For I do not know how far I am from being finally over this plague of desires. I much fear my secret sins, which Your eyes see when sometimes mine do not. In other temptations, I have some standard for examining myself. In this, I have scarce any. I can refrain in my thought life from the pleasures of the flesh and idle curiosity. I see my victories, when I reject these temptations. I reject and forgo the things that may be sin.

Then I ask myself how much more or less difficult it is that I do not have them. Desired wealth might cause me to partake in one or two or all of the three lusts.[12] If the soul cannot discern whether, when it has them, it hates them, they may be cast aside until a decision can be made. But to set aside praise is a harder matter. We either receive praise or we do not, so we have less power to decide whether to put ourselves in the way of it. To receive no praise we must live an incompetent life, abandoning all praiseworthy deeds and living atrociously. Then no one should think about us without despising. What greater madness than that can be said, or thought of? But if praise uses and ought to accompany a good life and good works, we ought to no more avoid its company than we do the company of a good life itself. Yet how do

I know whether I am handling something sinfully or in proper balance unless I am without it?

So what should I confess to You regarding how well I am standing against this temptation, O Lord? I confess that I am still delighted with praise, but more delighted with truth than with praise. If someone proposed that I could gain more favor with others if I would enter into frenzied error about truth, I would pass the test.

If I had a choice between a lie and being settled in a truth that would turn all people against me, I know how I would choose. I am of an opinion that the approbation of another should not increase my joy at doing what is right. Yet I admit that praise does give me joy and criticism diminishes my happiness. And when I am troubled of mind by the desire for praise, it occurs to me that this desire is excusable, for whatever that is worth. You know, God, for I am not certain.

The problem is that You have not simply commanded purity in regards to the objects of our affections. You also desire righteousness in how we bestow love upon both You and our neighbor as well. When I receive pleasing, intelligent praise, I seem to myself to be pleased with the thoughtfulness or compassion my neighbor is showing toward me. I am aggrieved when I see evil in another, when I hear him criticize what he doesn't understand or when he speaks against the good. Sometimes I am grieved at praise. It may come for something that I do not approve of and sometimes the thing praised seems to be held in higher esteem than it is worth.

But again, I am not in a good position to know how it is affecting me. I would not have him who praises me differ from me about myself because he is influenced by my concern for him. What passes for praiseworthy in my life to me might not please the other person as it does me. For some reason, I do not feel praised when my judgment of myself is not praised. As far as those things are praised that I dislike or they receive higher praise than I think they should, I feel less pleased with the praise. I come to doubt myself in this.

In You, O Truth, I see that I ought not to be moved at my own praises, for my own sake. Rather I should accept praise for the good of my neighbor. And whether that be my motivation, I am never sure. At this point I know less of myself than of You. I beseech You, O my God, to make it clear to me also. I want to confess to my brethren who pray for me where I find myself maimed. Let me examine myself again more diligently. If in my praise I am moved with the good of my neighbor, why am I less bothered if I hear another being unjustly criticized than if the criticism is directed at me? Why am I more stung by reproaches against myself, than if they are against another with equal injustice? Don't I know, or am I just trying to deceive myself and avoiding placing the truth before You in my heart and tongue?

Put this madness far from me, O Lord, lest my own mouth be the sinner's oil to make fat my head. I am poor and needy. Yet I am best, while I make hidden groanings because I am displeased with myself and know that I need

Your mercy. Then what is lacking in my defective state is better renewed and perfected. Then I can move on to that peace that the eye of the proud never knows.

❧

I have considered the sicknesses of my sins.
For that threefold lust I have called on You.
Stretch out Your right hand to help.
With wounded heart have I beheld Your brightness.
Stricken back by its light, I said, "Who can attain glory? I am cast away from Your eyes."
You are the Truth who preside over all.

But despite my covetousness, I would not willingly let go of You. But I would try to hold to You with the lie that I am well. Since no man can have Your presence in this way by falsehood, and I am not so ignorant of the truth, so I lost You. You will not allow Yourself to be possessed through a lie.

Whom could I find to reconcile me to You? Could I avail myself of angels or prayers or sacraments? Many who tried to return to You and found themselves unable have tried such means, or so I hear.

They tried to reach you through curious mystical visions. You considered them worthy—to be deluded. In their high-minded wanderings, they sought You by the pride of learning. They swelled their breasts instead of beating upon them. By the agreement of their heart, they drew unto themselves the princes of the air, the fellow-conspirators of their pride. Through their magical influences they were made fools. They sought a mediator, by whom they might be purged, and there was none.

It was the devil they found, transforming himself into an angel of light. And it much beguiled their proud flesh, that they found someone who had no body of flesh. For they were mortal sinners. But You, Lord, to whom they proudly sought to be reconciled, are immortal and without sin.

But for a mediator between God and man there must have something like to God and also something like to men. A mediator that was only like to man would be far from God. If he was only like to God, he would be too unlike man to mediate. That deceitful mediator then, by whom in your secret pride you deserved to be deluded, has only one thing in common with man. We share only sin. His spirit being would seem to have something in common with God, but without the ability to be clothed with mortal flesh, he only presumes upon immortality. The wages of sin is death. This he also has in common with men. With them he stands condemned to death.[13]

But the true Mediator appeared between mortal sinners and the immortal, Just One.[14] He is come in a secret mercy that You have showed to the humble. He was sent that by His example we might learn that same humility. There is one Mediator between God and man, the Man Christ Jesus. He is mortal with men. He is just with God. Because the wages of righteousness are life and peace, His righteousness conjoined with

God makes void that death of sinners, now made righteous. He willingly held His righteousness in common with them. Hence He was showed forth to holy men of old, that they through faith in His passion to come might be saved. We live through faith of the passion past. As Man, He was Mediator. As Word, He did not inhabit some middle ground between God and man. He was equal to God ... God with God ... together one God.

How have You loved us, good Father?

You spared not Your only Son.

You delivered Him up for us ungodly!

How have You loved us in Him?

His equality with You robbed You of no glory.

But You made Him submit even to the death of the cross.

He alone moved free among the dead.

He only had power to lay down His life.

He only had power to take it again.

Victor and Victim, and so Victor because Victim.

Priest and Sacrifice, and so Priest because Sacrifice.

Making of servants, sons, by being born of You and serving us.

Well then is my hope strong in Him that You will heal all my infirmities by Him Who sits at Your right hand and makes intercession for us. Otherwise I should despair, for many and great are my infirmities. As many and great as they are, Your medicine is more potent. We might imagine that Your Word was far from any union with man, and despair—unless He had been made flesh and dwelled among us.[15]

Frightened by my sins and weighed down by the burden of my misery, I had thrown away my heart and determined to flee to the wilderness. But You forbade me to leave and strenghtened me, saying, "Christ died for all, that they which live may now no longer live unto themselves, but unto Him that died for them."[16]

See, Lord, I cast my care upon You, that I may live, and consider wondrous things in Your law.[17] You know my ignorance and my sickness; teach me, and heal me. He Your only Son, in whom are hid all the treasures of wisdom and knowledge, hath redeemed me with His blood.[18] Let not the proud speak evil of me. I meditate on my ransom, and eat and drink, and communicate it. I would be one of the poor who are satisfied by Him.[19] I would be among those that eat and are satisfied, and they shall praise the Lord who seek Him.

Notes

1. From this confession of knowledge, Augustine moves to inquire by what faculty we can know God at all. He probes the mysterious character of the memory, wherein God is made known and dwells, but which could never discover Him.

2. Cf. 1 Corinthians 2:11.

3. These musings on self-knowledge and the knowledge of God relate to 1 Corinthians 13:8–13. While he does not speak in those terms, the understanding is that knowledge comes through faith, hope, and love, an epistemology that the Augustinian disciple John Calvin explores at length in Book 1 of *Institutes of the Christian Religion*.

4. Cf. 1 Corinthians 10:13.

5. Cf. Romans 1:20.

6. Cf. Luke 15:8–9.

7. This section rests heavily upon Augustine's contemplation and personal application of the thoughts of Paul in Romans 7:14–24 as he struggles with the "already" and the "not yet" of Christian existence. Paul's response of 8:1 that "there is now no condemnation for those who are in Christ Jesus" is seen by Augustine as more of a future hope, while sanctification remains a trial, a struggle against sin. Augustine echoes strains of Ecclesiastes as he wrestles with the enigma of the Christian's life in connection with God yet immersed in a fallen creation (cf. Rom. 8:8–24).

8. In the following discussion of new versus old affections, the guiding ideas from Scripture owe heavily to John's definition of sin in 1 John 2:16.

9. Athanasius of Alexandria (296–373) was the defender of orthodox faith against the Arians.

10. The central point toward which Augustine has been moving connects closely with Psalm 40, and he weaves a number of allusions to this psalm into the discussion of Christ's redemption from vanity.

11. Cf. Proverbs 3:34; Isaiah 64.

12. The three "lusts" mentioned here are apparently the three categories of 1 John 2:16: fleshly craving, lusts of the eyes, and pride or boasting.

13. Cf. Romans 6:23.

14. The controlling text for the following confession of Christ is Philippians 2:1–13.

15. Cf. John 1:14.

16. Cf. Romans 5:6–8.

17. Cf. Psalm 119:18–20.

18. Cf. Colossians 2:1–3.

19. Cf. Psalm 22:26.

The Heaven and the Earth

"In the beginning, You made heaven and earth."

Moses told us this; he wrote and departed. He passed hence from You to You. Nor is he now before me. If he were, I would grab hold of him and ask him about this. I would beg him by You to open more of these mysteries. I would dedicate the ears of my body to the sounds bursting out of his mouth. Should he speak Hebrew, in vain will it strike my senses. None of it could touch my mind. But if Latin, I should know what he said.

But how should I know, whether he spoke truth? And if I knew this also, should I know from him how he received the truth? Truly within me, in the chamber of my thoughts, Truth is neither Hebrew, nor Greek, nor Latin, nor a foreign tongue. Were I to hear Moses in any language, my mind without organs of voice or tongue or sound of syllables, would say, "It is truth."

I should say confidently to that man of Yours, "You are telling me the truth."

Since I cannot inquire of Moses, it is You, O Truth, that I ask for knowledge. It was Your truth that Moses was full of when he spoke truth. Forgive my sins, my God, I ask. Then give to me to understand, as You gave to this servant.

Behold, the heavens and the earth exist. Existence proclaims that they were created, even in their changes and variations. Anything that is yet has not been made, has nothing in it that it did not have before. If a noncreated being could be, it could not change and vary. Creation itself proclaims that things did not make themselves: "We are, because we have been made. We were not therefore, before we were, so as to make ourselves."

Now the evidence of the thing is the voice of the speakers:

You therefore, Lord, made them.

You are beautiful, for they are beautiful.

You are good, for they are good.

You are, for they are.

Yet they are not beautiful nor good, nor are they, as You their Creator are. Compared with You, they are neither beautiful, nor good, nor are.

This we know.

Thanks be to You.

And our knowledge, compared with Your knowledge, is ignorance.

But how did You make the heaven and the earth? What was the engine of Your mighty fabric? For it was not as a human craftsman, forming one body from another, according to the wisdom of his mind.

Human understanding can in some way make form according to an idea that is first seen by the inward eye. The craftsman should have no mental pictures to form unless You had made that mind. He draws on ideas from forms that already exist and have being, whether they are made from clay or stone or wood or gold or something else. And how should forms be, if You did not first decide upon them? You made the body even of the craftsman. You the mind commanded his limbs into existence. You formed the matter whereof he makes anything. You gave his mind the apprehension whereby to take in his art and interpret inside the mind Your world without. The senses You gave to his body help him translate mental image into the reality he creates. The senses are exterior to the mind, yet they can go within to consult the truth that presides over the creation, whether it be well done or not.

All these praise You, the Creator of all. But how do You make them? How, O God, did You make heaven and earth? Neither in the heaven nor in the earth did You make heaven and earth. You did not have for Your workshop the air or waters, since these also belong to the heaven and the earth. No place in the whole world did You make the whole world. There was no place to make it, before it was made, that it might be. Nor did You hold raw matter in Your hand from which to fashion heaven and earth. Where would you get something You did not make from which to make anything? For can anything be, except that You are? You spoke, and they were made. In Your Word You made them.

But how did You speak? Was it in the way that the voice came out of the cloud, saying, "This is my beloved Son"?[1] For that voice passed by and its sounds faded. Its words began and ended. The tones sounded and passed away, one after another, until the last became silence. It seems clear from the abundantly plain account that these words found their source in the motion of one of Your creatures. The temporal expresses temporal words to serve Your eternal will.

And these Your words, created for a time, were reported by the outward ear to the intelligent soul, whose inward ear lay listening to Your Eternal Word. But the ear compared the sounds of these words with that Your Eternal Word spoke in silence.

The eternal Word said, "The sounds you now hear are different, far different. These words are far beneath me, nor do they have final being. These words flee and pass away. But the Word abides over all things forever."

If it had been in temporal words that You commanded heaven and earth to be made, and so it was, there would have necessarily been a corporeal creature before heaven and earth. This mediator of sound would have had to give motion in time to Your eternal voice. In so doing, the authority of the commands might find fulfillment in time in the voice.

But we see no reference to anything corporeal before heaven and earth. If there were, surely You had no need of such a passing voice to create.[2] Also, Your first command would have had to be to make this voice by which to say, "Let the heaven and the earth be made." For there was nothing by which to make the voice unless You made it. Without Your power it could not be at all. By what Word did You speak into existence a body before there was a universe to make those words?

You call us to understand the Word,

God with God, Word spoken eternally.

By the eternal Word were all things spoken eternally.

For what was spoken was not sound after sound.

There was no consecutive march of noises,

from sound concluded to the next voiced.

No, all things were spoken together.

All things were spoken eternally.

Were it not so, we would still have time and change, but we could not have a true eternity or true immortality. This I know, O my God, and for it I give thanks. I know things, Lord, I confess to You with blessing and thanksgiving, as do all others who find assurance in the truth.

We know, Lord, we know, inasmuch as we know of things that once were and no longer have existence. From our perspective, not Yours, things do not exist that once did. Things now exist that once did not. Things die and arise. But it is not that Your Word is giving place to one thing and then replacing it later with something else. For Your Word truly is immortal and eternal.

Therefore You say once and forever what You say by the Word that exists. Its being is in Your eternal command. What You said would exist finds its existence at the time You set. Nor do You make anything except by the Word of Your power in the creation decree.

What is comes along in the time of Your choosing, though existing things hold their being in the decree You issued in the everlasting times. It was in the eternal now that You made all things together and made them by the Word.

Help me understand this, I beseech You, O Lord. What I can see of it seems difficult to express.

Much I do not understand, unless it is that all things exist at once in Your eternal reason, where it is "now." I see things begin to be and stop being, then begin again and stop again. But I am seeing from a fixed point within Your eternal now. For You all is a single moment, but You plan for our standpoint, from which things ought to begin and end. In Your reason, nothing really begins or ends.

This is Your Word, which was also the beginning and now speaks to us. In the gospel He spoke in the flesh.

This Word sounded outwardly in the ears of men, that it might be believed and sought inwardly and found to be the eternal truth. In this truth, the good and only Master teaches all His disciples. And now, Lord, I hear You speaking to me. The One who teaches us now speaks to us. But a man who does not teach us, even though He speaks, does not speak to us. Who teaches us? Only the unchangeable Truth.

We can be admonished by a changeable creature. But the best a man can do is lead us to the unchangeable Truth. That is the only place where we can truly stand and hear and learn. It is the only place to hear the Bridegroom's voice and rejoice. The Truth alone can reconcile us to Him to whom we belong.

We must return to the beginning. Unless this stable point still existed, we would have no place to return to after we wandered off. In order to find our way back from error, we must know, and we only can know because there is an eternal Word. He alone teaches us, because He alone is the beginning, and in Him alone can the beginning speak to us.

In this Beginning, O God, have You made heaven and earth.

In Your Word,
In Your Son,
In Your Power,
In Your Wisdom,
In Your Truth.
Wondrously You spoke and wondrously made.

Who shall comprehend? Who declare it?

What is it that gleams through me?

What strikes my heart without hurt?

What makes me shudder and glow, impassioned?

This force is so unlike me, so I shudder.

But this force is what I was made to be like, so I ignite.

Here is Wisdom, Wisdom shines through me, dispelling the fog that still folds its mantle about me. I faint in the dark from trying to bear my punishment. My strength is ebbing away in my great need. I have come to the point that I cannot support my blessings.

It is at this extremity, Lord, that you come in grace to lift away my sins and heal my diseases. For You will also redeem my life from corruption, and crown me with loving kindness and tender mercies, and will satisfy my desire with good things, because my youth shall be renewed like an eagle's.[3] For in hope we are saved, so we wait patiently for the fullness of Your promises.

Let him who is able turn an inward ear to hear You as I boldly cry out from Your oracle, "How many are your works, O Lord! In wisdom you made them all."[4]

This Wisdom is the Beginning, and in that Beginning Your eternal Word makes heaven and earth.

Hear now the silliness of those full of their old sin nature, who scoff and ask us, "What was God doing before He made heaven and earth?" They continue in this vein, "If He were unemployed and did nothing, why does He have to stay occupied forever after now? Why can't He keep doing nothing as He did before? Did God develop some new motion or suddenly wish to make a creature, although He had never had the urge to do it before?"

How would such a line of reasoning fit what must happen in a real eternity? Is the eternal God going to find a wish that He has previously lacked? The will of God is not a creature to be formed in His thinking. God's will was before and underlies every creature. Nothing could have been created unless the will of the Creator preceded the act. The will of a Creator must then belong to His very Substance. And if anything arose from a new act of will that was not always there, then the substance of God cannot be described as changelessly eternal.

"Well," another might counter, "if the will of God has been from eternity that the creature should be, then the creature is from eternity."

Anyone who would say something like this does not yet understand You, O divine Wisdom that is the Light of souls. Such a one does not yet understand what creation means in relation to the Creator. With such superficialities, people strive to understand eternal truth while the heart flutters between thoughts of time past, present, and future. This view of time is essentially unstable. Can we grab hold of this idea of time in flux and repair it, so that the heart will settle down enough to catch a glimpse of the glory of a fixed eternity?

For eternity by definition is fixed and cannot be compared to the moments we experience, which are never fixed. How do we know that a long time has become long? We sense the passing by of many motions and changes. Were there no motions or changes, there would be no length of movements to call "time." In the eternal realm the whole must be present. In our minds, we cannot imagine time in that totality now. For us, all time past is driven on by time to come, and all to come follows upon the past. But in God's timetable of creation, all past and future are one design, flowing out of one now.

Who shall hold the heart of man still enough to see how eternity stands still, without time past or to come? Who can explain times past and future? Can my hand hold the heart still? Can my mouth by speech bring about a thing so great?

So someone asks, "What did God do before He made heaven and earth?" I would not answer flippantly that "He was preparing hell for those who pry into mysteries." That would set aside the gravity of the question. It is one thing to answer inquiries and another to make sport of inquirers. That is not a proper way to answer. It is better to respond, "I do not know" regarding matters that lie ultimately beyond our imagination, than to poke fun at the one who brings up deep things. Nor should we give praise to one who invents answers to hide what he doesn't know.

What I can say is that You, our God, made every creature. But if under the category "heaven and earth" *every* creature is meant, I would boldly say that before God made heaven and earth, He did not make anything. For if He did make something, what He made was a creature.

I do not have all the information that it might be to my benefit to know, but I am sure that no creature was made before there was made any creature.

It is an irrelevance to wander over imaginary ideas of precreation past, and wonder why You, the all-creating God almighty, did for innumerable ages put off so great a work as making heaven and earth.

Let this dreamer wake and consider that such wondering is a silly conceit. For from what source did these innumerable ages come that passed by before You made ages? Aren't You also the Author and Creator of all ages? What times should there be that were not made by You? How should they pass if they had no objective existence? Seeing that You are the Creator of all times, if any time was before You made heaven and earth, then how can they say that You were not at work? You had to have made it. That very time would have found its being in You. Nor could each moment of that time have passed by unless You had prepared the next moment to replace it.

If before heaven and earth came to be there was no time, why should anyone demand to know how You were passing Your time then? Without time, there was no "then."

Your Being does not inhabit passing moments, so You did not precede time in time. Otherwise You Yourself would not have existed before time. You surely do precede all things past in the majesty of an ever-present eternity; and surpass all that to us exists in future. To us, the future will come and go. To You it is as much now as this moment.

You surely do not change from now to then.

Your years do not fail nor come or go, while ours must.

Each of ours must follow until all make an appearance.

Your years stand together because they stand in one.

Not one is thrust aside by the following.

So they cannot pass away when ours are no more.

Your years are one day.

Your day is only today.

Your today makes no room for a tomorrow.

It does not replace any yesterdays.

Your today is eternity.[5]

In this sense only did You beget The Coeternal, to whom You said, "This day have I begotten You." But as One You have made all things; and before all times You are. At no time was there no time in Your existence.

At no time then had You not made anything, because time itself was part of what You made. So it is perhaps wrong to say that times are coeternal with You. Better to say that You abide in the fullness of Your being.

I posit that we should not think of Your mode of existence as time. For what is time? Who can readily and briefly explain this? Who can even in thought comprehend it, so as to utter a word about it? But think how often we refer to time with such knowing familiarity when we talk to each other. And, we understand, when we speak of it, a part of what it means. We can make meaningful ideas around it when we hear another speak of it.

But I repeat: What then is time? So long as no one asks me, I know what it is. If I wish to explain it to one that asks, I suddenly find I do not really know. Yet I say boldly that I know some things. If nothing ever passed away then it would be wrong to speak of time past. If nothing were coming in the following pieces of existence there would be no future. And if nothing were native to now, there would be no present. Those two times then, past and future— what can we say about their existence: the past-now things have no existence nor do the future now things? All we have are the things of the present-now. If the present remained one present always and never passed into time past, truly it should not be time. It would be eternity.

If time present is only time because it exists and then passes into time past, how can we say that there is a present? It only exists in order that it might move into former existence. So one reason we cannot truly say that time is, is because it is continually tending not to be.

And yet we refer to "a long time" and "a short time," thinking of time past or to come. We say that something happened a long time past, meaning that a hundred of our years has come and gone since the moment in question. Something a long time in the future may mean a hundred years from now.

A short time past, we call it when it happened ten days ago, and something is expected to occur in a short time if it is ten days from now.

In what sense is that long or short, since neither events of the past or future have objective reality to our "now"? The past is disconnected from us by what did exist and no longer does. The future is not yet.

To be accurate we should not say that something happened long ago, but rather "It has been long." Of the future, "It will be long."

O my Lord, my Light, doesn't Your Truth mock our simple reasonings? For that past time which was so "long," was it long when it was past or before it was past, when it was present? It might have been long, when it happened, but now that it is past it is no longer long. The time period no longer is long. It has no existence at all. So we should not then say, "That time in the past was long." We shall not find it or find what was long about it, for it is no more. But let us say, "That present time was long." When it was the present time, it did seem long. When it was present it had not yet passed away until it ceased to be. Therefore there was a succession of moments that could be described as long, but this is no longer the case, now that those moments are past and have ceased to be long or short or anything else.

Let us see then, soul of man, whether present time can be long. To our consciousness a sense has been given to be aware of time and able to measure its length. But how will you answer me in judgment of time? Is a hundred years, while it is present, a long time? Can a hundred years be present? If the first of these years is current, that much of it is present, but the other ninety and nine not in existence to us. If the second year is current, one year is now past, another present, and the rest are to come. If we assume any year in the midst of the hundred to be present, then the rest are either before or after. So a hundred years cannot be present.

But can the one year of the hundred which is now current be present? For if the first of its months is current, the rest are still to come. If it is the second month, then the first is already past, and the rest are not yet. Therefore, not even the current year can be described as "present" as a whole. For twelve months make up a year; of which one must be the current month and the rest either past or future.

See that we can take this on, for neither is the current month all present, since we are living only one day of it. The rest of the days are to come if we are on the first day of the month. If it is the last day, all are past. If it is in the middle, some are past and some future.

See how the present time, which alone we found could be called long, is abridged to the length of scarcely one day. And let us examine that as well. We are not living an entire day as a whole right now. It is made up of twenty-four hours of night and day. At the first hour, the rest are to come; at the last most are past. In the middle, some are past and some future. And even that one hour passes away in flying particles. Whatsoever of it has flown away, is past; whatsoever remains, is to come.

If an instant of time be conceived, which cannot be divided into the smallest particles of moments, that alone is what can properly be called present. Instants fly by at such speed from future to past that one of them cannot be long enough that we are aware of it. For if a moment was long enough to be contemplated, it would be long enough to divide into past and future. The present truly has no space between what was and what will be.

Where then is the time that we may call "long"? Is it to come? We cannot say it is long, because it is not yet in existence. We can only say, "It will be long." When therefore will it be? For if even then, when it is yet to come, it shall not be long (because what can be long, as yet does not exist). It shall only be long, when it has appeared out of the future and has begun to be. Then it will have started to become the present. But when it is present it will not be in existence long enough to regard in any accurate sense as "long." It would seem that time cries out with the above explanation that it cannot be long.

Notes

1. Cf. Matthew 3:17; 17:5; Mark 1:11; Luke 3:22.
2. Cf. John 1:3; Revelation 4:9–11. Related to Christ as Creator, see Colossians 1:16–20.
3. Cf. Psalm 103:1–5.
4. Psalm 104:24.
5. "For Where the day neither commences with the end of yesterday, nor is ended by the commencement of the morrow, it is ever today." (*Enchiridion* 49).

The Living Soul

All things are fair that You have made, but I can see well enough to tell that You Yourself are unutterably fairer in that You made such things. Had Adam not fallen, the ocean of brackishness would never have flowed out of him to despoil everything. As it is, the human race is profoundly curious, and its waves are tempestuous, with swelling and restless tumbling to and fro.

Had there been no fall, there would be no need for You to bring those who dispense Your grace to work in the many waters of sinful thoughts. You call them to do much of their work in a material manner, applying the senses. But You also use more spiritual doings and saying. In the ocean there are both crawling and soaring beings. You lead us like that. Material sacraments aid us to be initiated and consecrated. But these things in themselves would benefit no one. We also need leadership for the spiritual life. After the word of admission, we must move forward toward completion.

So it is in Your Word that we can leave the depths of the shifting sea currents and live on land, separate from the bitter waters. We can experience life, not as the moving creatures of the waters but as the living soul that walks the earth.

Once on land we are beyond the need of baptism, though the unbelievers do have need until washed in the waters that lead to the only entrance of the kingdom of heaven that You have made.

The soul no longer needs to wander about seeking after miracles or other wonderful things to believe in. For true faith is not like that. It doesn't need a steady diet of signs and wonders in order to believe, now that the faithful earth is separated from the waters that were bitter with infidelity. Tongues are for a sign, not to them that believe, but to them that believe not. Neither then does that earth You have founded upon the waters need the flying animals that at Your word the waters brought forth.

Send You Your word into the world by Your messengers. We can talk about what they accomplish, but You do the work in them in such a way that You work as their living souls work in the task.

The earth brings it forth, because the earth is the cause that they work in the soul, as the sea was the cause that they wrought upon the moving creatures that have life, and the fowls that fly under the firmament of heaven, of whom the earth has no need; although it feeds upon that fish which was taken out of the deep, upon that table which You have prepared in the presence of them that believe. For therefore was He taken out of the deep, that He might feed the dry land; and the fowl, though bred in the sea, is yet multiplied upon the earth. For of the first preaching of the Evangelists, man's infidelity was the cause; yet are the faithful also exhorted and blessed by them openly from day to day. But the living soul takes his beginning from the earth: for it profits only those already among the Faithful to contain themselves from the love of this world, that so their soul may live unto You, which was dead while it lived in pleasures; in death-bringing pleasures, Lord, for You, Lord, are the life-giving delight of the pure heart.

Let Your ministers work upon the earth, not as upon the waters of faithless preaching and speaking in signs and sacraments and mysticism. In this swamp, ignorance breeds misplaced admiration. Attention is set upon the men out of awe of their secret signs. Such is the way to faith that the sons of Adam still would rather find and forget You and find an alternative. All the while they hide from Your face, and become like the dark depths of the sea.

But let Your ministers work who stand with the sure-footedness of standing on dry land. Keep them away from the whirlpools that suck into the great deep. Make them a pattern to the Faithful by living before them, and stirring them up to imitation. For that is the way that people hear, but then go beyond hearing to doing.

Seek the Lord, and your soul shall live, that the earth may bring forth the living soul.

◈

O Lord God, give us peace, for You have given us all things.

Give us the peace of rest, the peace of a sabbath without evening.

For a most wondrous array of things all around us is very good.

But things finish their time and pass away.

In everything but You there is morning and evening.

◈

GRATIAS TIBI DOMINE